Cooperative Learning in Undergraduate Mathematics

Issues That Matter
and
Strategies That Work

ISBN: 0-88385-166-0

Library of Congress Catalog Card Number 00-111025

Printed in the United States of America

Current Printing

10 9 8 7 6 5 4 3 2 1

Cooperative Learning in Undergraduate Mathematics

Issues That Matter and Strategies That Work

Written by

Participants in Project CLUME
(Cooperative Learning in Undergraduate Mathematics Education)

Edited by

Elizabeth C. Rogers
Piedmont College

Barbara E. Reynolds
Cardinal Stritch University

Neil A. Davidson
University of Maryland

Anthony D. Thomas
University of Wisconsin-Platteville

Published and Distributed by
The Mathematical Association of America

The MAA Notes Series, started in 1982, addresses a broad range of topics and themes of interest to all who are involved with undergraduate mathematics. The volumes in this series are readable, informative, and useful, and help the mathematical community keep up with developments of importance to mathematics.

MAA Notes

11. Keys to Improved Instruction by Teaching Assistants and Part-Time Instructors, *Committee on Teaching Assistants and Part-Time Instructors, Bettye Anne Case,* Editor.

13. Reshaping College Mathematics, *Committee on the Undergraduate Program in Mathematics, Lynn A. Steen,* Editor.

14. Mathematical Writing, by *Donald E. Knuth, Tracy Larrabee, and Paul M. Roberts.*

16. Using Writing to Teach Mathematics, *Andrew Sterrett,* Editor.

17. Priming the Calculus Pump: Innovations and Resources, *Committee on Calculus Reform and the First Two Years,* a subcommittee of the Committee on the Undergraduate Program in Mathematics, *Thomas W. Tucker,* Editor.

18. Models for Undergraduate Research in Mathematics, *Lester Senechal,* Editor.

19. Visualization in Teaching and Learning Mathematics, *Committee on Computers in Mathematics Education, Steve Cunningham and Walter S. Zimmermann,* Editors.

20. The Laboratory Approach to Teaching Calculus, *L. Carl Leinbach et al.,* Editors.

21. Perspectives on Contemporary Statistics, *David C. Hoaglin and David S. Moore,* Editors.

22. Heeding the Call for Change: Suggestions for Curricular Action, *Lynn A. Steen,* Editor.

24. Symbolic Computation in Undergraduate Mathematics Education, *Zaven A. Karian,* Editor.

25. The Concept of Function: Aspects of Epistemology and Pedagogy, *Guershon Harel and Ed Dubinsky,* Editors.

26. Statistics for the Twenty-First Century, *Florence and Sheldon Gordon,* Editors.

27. Resources for Calculus Collection, Volume 1: Learning by Discovery: A Lab Manual for Calculus, *Anita E. Solow,* Editor.

28. Resources for Calculus Collection, Volume 2: Calculus Problems for a New Century, *Robert Fraga,* Editor.

29. Resources for Calculus Collection, Volume 3: Applications of Calculus, *Philip Straffin,* Editor.

30. Resources for Calculus Collection, Volume 4: Problems for Student Investigation, *Michael B. Jackson and John R. Ramsay,* Editors.

31. Resources for Calculus Collection, Volume 5: Readings for Calculus, *Underwood Dudley,* Editor.

32. Essays in Humanistic Mathematics, *Alvin White,* Editor.

33. Research Issues in Undergraduate Mathematics Learning: Preliminary Analyses and Results, *James J. Kaput and Ed Dubinsky,* Editors.

34. In Eves' Circles, *Joby Milo Anthony,* Editor.

35. You're the Professor, What Next? Ideas and Resources for Preparing College Teachers, *The Committee on Preparation for College Teaching, Bettye Anne Case,* Editor.

36. Preparing for a New Calculus: Conference Proceedings, *Anita E. Solow,* Editor.

37. A Practical Guide to Cooperative Learning in Collegiate Mathematics, *Nancy L. Hagelgans, Barbara E. Reynolds, SDS, Keith Schwingendorf, Draga Vidakovic, Ed Dubinsky, Mazen Shahin, G. Joseph Wimbish, Jr.*

38. Models That Work: Case Studies in Effective Undergraduate Mathematics Programs, *Alan C. Tucker,* Editor.

39. Calculus: The Dynamics of Change, *CUPM Subcommittee on Calculus Reform and the First Two Years, A. Wayne Roberts,* Editor.

40. Vita Mathematica: Historical Research and Integration with Teaching, *Ronald Calinger,* Editor.

MAA Service Center
P. O. Box 91112
Washington, DC 20090-1112
800-331-1622   fax: 301-206-9789

Preface

Until recently (say, 20 or 30 years ago), lecture had been the predominant mode of delivery for undergraduate mathematics classes. Since the Tulane conference in 1986 calling for a lean and lively calculus and the first call from the National Science Foundation in 1988 for proposals addressing changes in the calculus curriculum, discussions of undergraduate mathematics education have included a variety of small-group and active learning strategies. Early research in cooperative learning was focused on the pre-college level (both elementary and high school students). The climate and possibilities in undergraduate classrooms—whether at institutions with a majority of traditional-aged students coming directly from high schools or at institutions serving a majority of returning-adult students—are significantly different from those in pre-college schools. The challenges of implementing any kind of pedagogical strategies beyond the traditional lecture are different in undergraduate mathematics classrooms from those in other settings. Among any group of faculty discussing undergraduate mathematics education, there will be those who espouse some kind of small-group or active learning strategies. Cooperative learning is one pedagogical model that has attracted much attention in recent years.

Since 1995, nearly 150 mathematics faculty have participated in MAA Project CLUME (Cooperative Learning in Undergraduate Mathematics Education) Workshops. Project CLUME included intensive summer immersion workshops, an ongoing support system for CLUME participants, and reports from the participants on how they implemented cooperative learning in the first year following their experience in the summer workshop. In June 1996, a group of about two dozen of the CLUME-95 workshop participants gathered at Purdue University for a reunion workshop. In discussing their experiences—both triumphs and trials—in implementing cooperative learning in a variety of situations, they realized that they had much to offer to the wider community of undergraduate mathematics faculty.

The authors of this volume, while acknowledging that there are a variety of effective pedagogical strategies, are strongly committed to cooperative learning. When it works, cooperative learning has been shown to be at least as effective as other pedagogical strategies for promoting student achievement in mathematics. Several of the authors are actively engaged in research projects exploring why cooperative learning is effective and how it can be made more effective. All of the authors have used cooperative learning in significant ways in their own classrooms for several years.

This volume has been nearly four years in preparation. During this time, each chapter has been written and re-written by small groups of authors, then critiqued by the larger group. As often happens in an extended project of this kind, some of the original participants of the project dropped out, and several other colleagues joined. Most of the 17 authors of this volume were participants in the first Project CLUME Workshop held at Purdue University in July 1995, one was a participant in the CLUME-97 Workshop held at Georgia State University in June 1997, and three began using cooperative learning following Calculus, Computers and Cooperative Learning Workshops held at Purdue University in the summers of 1991 and 1992.

Several perspectives on cooperative learning in undergraduate mathematics in this volume have not appeared anywhere else, and a number of features make this volume unique.

In this volume, the authors provide practical suggestions and strategies for experienced instructors who are already implementing cooperative learning in their classes as well as materials helpful for beginning or experienced instructors who are thinking about incorporating cooperative learning strategies in their classes. Perspectives from many implementers of cooperative learning are presented—not just the authors of this volume. These have been gleaned from a survey conducted by Project CLUME participants among 94 of our colleagues. This survey with the responses that were received are included in an Appendix to this volume.

The first chapter gives a historical overview of cooperative learning. It focuses on ways that cooperative and collaborative learning strategies have been used in undergraduate mathematics classes to meet a variety of different needs. After a very brief overview of theoretical distinctions in the field of small-group learning, several examples of large-scale implementations of cooperative learning are presented. These few examples provide the reader ample evidence that there are a variety of ways to use cooperative learning so that it is effective for student learning. These examples also illustrate that cooperative learning is being implemented, even institutionalized, in large-scale ways at some colleges and universities.

There is an entire chapter (Chapter 2) on practical ways to develop a social climate conducive to cooperative learning in the classroom. This chapter deals also with other practical issues of implementation including: how to get started, how to physically arrange the room, how to form groups and how long to keep them together, how to attend to issues of group dynamics in order to build a positive group climate, and how to prevent or resolve difficulties within and among the groups.

Many examples of cooperative strategies, which the authors have used in their own classes, are described in Chapter 3. Specific examples are given for ways to use each strategy in such courses as elementary statistics, the mathematics courses for elementary education majors, college algebra, precalculus, calculus, discrete mathematics, abstract algebra, and topology. Each strategy is presented with a description, some typical uses, and several mathematical examples.

Concerns about evaluating individual student achievement in a cooperative learning environment are considered in Chapter 4. The authors present a conceptual model for assessment and discuss grading and related issues. Assessment strategies are examined in a way that acknowledges that grades, for undergraduates, are both motivational and evaluative. A variety of assessment strategies are presented, including both formal evaluative strategies which contribute directly to a student's course grade, and informal strategies that help to guide instructional decisions from day to day.

The authors of Chapter 5 believe that they can use what they know about how people learn mathematics to design activities for cooperative learning. Four general categories of theories relating the nature of mathematical content to views of the role of a mathematics educator in helping students learn that content are presented. Examples are developed that illustrate how a teacher might construct cooperative learning activities for a particular lesson based on his particular beliefs about the nature of mathematics and how mathematics is learned. In the final section of the chapter, the role that formal research on learning can play in informing the design of instruction is considered.

In writing this volume, the authors found they had to clarify, compare, and contrast the distinctive approaches each was using to incorporate cooperative learning in different ways. In Chapter 6 they present some of their emerging understanding of fundamental differences in our various approaches to cooperative learning. Several different instructors' stories of their use of cooperative learning illustrate how different beliefs about learning and teaching help to shape teaching practice in abstract algebra, developmental algebra, college algebra, and statistics classes.

Practical ideas for conducting introductory faculty development workshops for undergraduate mathematics faculty are offered in Chapter 7. This chapter provides outlines for one-hour, two-hour, and half-day workshops as well as a two-day mini-course on cooperative learning in mathematics. Elaboration of the outlines includes substantial detail about the major topics, sequence, and flow of such a workshop.

The Bibliography provides a number of the major references available in the field of cooperative learning in mathematics education. To make this bibliography easier to use, it has been arranged in two sections. The first section is the usual bibliography including references cited throughout the text and some sources for further reading. The second section lists a selection of some textbooks and course materials that the authors have found work well in a cooperative classroom for undergraduate mathematics students.

This project has been an unusual experience of collaboration for those of us involved in producing this volume. Each of the chapters has been written collaboratively, and all of us have participated in critiquing and revising the entire volume. In addition to the 17 authors, we acknowledge the work of the committee who developed and conducted the Survey on Cooperative Learning to determine some current practices and experiences with cooperative learning in the mathematics classroom. Bernadette Baker, Nancy Hagelgans, Ieda Rodrigues, and Varona Wynn adapted the Survey that had been used by the authors of *A Practical Guide to Cooperative Learning in Collegiate Mathematics* (MAA Notes Series, Volume 37). This revised Survey, called the CLUME Survey, was made available in three versions with identical questions. Those responding could request a hard copy to be returned by U. S. mail, or they could complete an email version. Subsequently, John Lavin, a senior computer science major at Ursinus College, developed an interactive version for the World Wide Web.

Bernadette Baker, Nancy Hagelgans, and Ieda Rodrigues used lists of participants in Calculus, Computers and Cooperative Learning workshops held at Purdue University for several summers beginning in 1991. Cooperative learning had been both a pedagogical feature of those workshops and a topic of study by the participants. This committee sent invitations to respond to the survey to all those participants who had current addresses in the Combined Membership List as well as to a few other colleagues known to be interested in cooperative learning. Some of these invitations were returned unopened, but 423 invitations, 279 via email and 144 via U. S. mail, apparently reached their intended destinations. About 20 people responded to say that they were not answering the survey because they were not using cooperative learning; some of these people were retired. By mid-July, after an email reminder had been sent, there were 94 responses. Of these, 17 were hard copy, 12 were email messages, and the remainder were World Wide Web responses. Some respondents fully answered questions at the beginning of the survey but did not answer the later questions; their answers are included, as far as they went, in the final results. We are grateful to Margie Connor, a secretary at Ursinus College, who helped to organize the data so that all responses to each question appeared together.

Throughout this volume, we discuss the results of the CLUME Survey where the topics are related to particular questions. In a very concrete way, this volume reflects not only the experiences of the authors, but also those of the CLUME Survey respondents.

Beyond this, we acknowledge the invaluable support of the participants, faculty, and staff of MAA's Project CLUME Workshops that were held on the campuses of Purdue University and Georgia State University, the support of the National Science Foundation (NSF DUE 94-55164 and NSF DUE 96-53383), and the personal support of our colleagues, friends, and families without whom this volume would not have come to be.

Table of Contents

Chapter 1

Introduction to Cooperative Learning in Undergraduate Mathematics

Neil A. Davidson, Barbara E. Reynolds, Elizabeth C. Rogers

Cooperation in Human Affairs

Cooperation is a long-standing concept in human affairs, and indeed it is known to be essential to the functioning of human groups, organizations, and societies. What does it mean to cooperate or to collaborate? Examining a variety of dictionaries, we see that to cooperate means to work or act together or jointly and to unite in producing an effect. Cooperation involves joint operation or action, and the term "cooperation" also has social, economic, and biological interpretations. For instance, the social meaning of cooperation is an activity shared for mutual benefit. The economic meaning of cooperation is a combination of persons working together for purposes of production, purchase, or distribution. The biological/ecological meaning of cooperation is the conscious or unconscious behavior of organisms living together that produces a result with survival value. Collaboration is a specific form of cooperation. According to many dictionaries, to collaborate means to work jointly with one or a limited number of others in a project such as a written or artistic composition or research.

While cooperation in education may appear to be a twentieth-century development, it has long-standing roots in many societies. For example, an ancient Hebrew tradition suggests having a partner with whom one can discuss and dispute in the study of a sacred text such as the *Talmud*. Yet it has only

been in the twentieth-century that we can see systematic and wide-ranging international research and development of the key concepts and methods related to cooperation in education. These methods, when applied in the classroom, are typically known as either cooperative learning or collaborative learning.

Cooperative Learning Approaches

Cooperative learning approaches are forms of active learning that engage students in working and learning together in small groups, typically with two to five members. Cooperative learning strategies are designed to engage students actively in the learning process through inquiry and discussions with their classmates. Group work is carefully organized to promote the participation and learning of all group members in a jointly shared task or learning activity. Students work together for varied purposes: to share and discuss their ideas, to think and reason critically and creatively, to discuss concepts and principles, to practice skills or master information, to apply theories or techniques in a real-life setting, to carry out an investigation, or to create a group product or performance.

Some of the research literature makes a distinction between "cooperative learning" and "collaborative learning." However, in this present

1

work, we will not focus on the distinctions; rather we will present commonalities and a variety of ways that these approaches to learning are being implemented in undergraduate mathematics. Unless stated otherwise, the reader may assume that we are using the terms "cooperate" and "collaborate" interchangeably.

There is considerable diversity in the field of cooperative learning, and no single guru is accepted on all points. The field has a number of diverse viewpoints, which can result in arguments over which approach is better or more correct. However, diversity can be viewed as a source of strength in terms of flexibility and mutually enriching perspectives. The many approaches to cooperative and collaborative learning that have several points in common and a range of differences and variations. All approaches have more similarities than differences.

For example, one afternoon as several of the authors were working together, discussing and revising Chapter 6 (in which several distinct examples of our implementations of cooperative learning are presented), one of us observed, "You keep saying here that your students discover these ideas, but that's not what you actually describe happening in your classroom. You seem to be guiding your students toward constructing ideas and concepts rather than have the students discover them." This conversation led to a realization among ourselves that the authors of this volume have broadly differing perspectives on the purpose of group work and cooperative learning activities in our classes. In Davidson's original work (1971) discovery is the whole point of the activities, while for Reynolds the activities give the students an opportunity to think very hard about mathematical ideas. If the students engage seriously in the introductory activities, she finds them better prepared for a follow-up lecture-discussion in which the mathematical concepts are presented, even if they do not get the right answers at first. This conversation led us to a realization that the small group discovery method of Davidson (see Chapter 6) and the action-process-object-schema (APOS) theory of Dubinsky and his collaborators (see Chapter 5) generate distinctly different approaches to cooperative learning in collegiate mathematics.

Using cooperative learning strategies is not merely a matter of suggesting that the students get together and work in groups. Rather, the instructor

who uses cooperative learning plays a very active role in structuring the learning environment for the class. If the instructor is tentative in suggesting that students collaborate, their collaboration will be tentative. Some have suggested that cooperative learning strategies bring about a shift in the role of the instructor—from acting as a sage on the stage to serving as a guide on the side. While this is true to a certain extent, the authors of this volume have found that using cooperative learning in our undergraduate mathematics classes requires that the instructor take a proactive role in the classroom in order to set the climate for effective and productive group learning. The instructor sets the tone for cooperation, plans the lesson and introduces it to the class, sets up class activities and homework, facilitates group work, and helps students reflect on their interactions and learning experiences. Throughout the rest of this volume, these aspects of the instructor's role are discussed as the authors share their experiences in implementing cooperative learning in their own classrooms.

Why Use Cooperative Learning in Mathematics?

There are many reasons for using small groups in mathematics classes. Small groups offer a social support mechanism for the learning of mathematics. Students in small groups can help one another master basic information and procedures in the context of more meaningful problems. Small-group learning offers opportunities for all students to succeed in mathematics.

Learning can be a social activity, and mathematics is filled with exciting and challenging ideas for discussion. Students can learn by talking, listening, explaining, and thinking with others. Students are often able to explain ideas to one another using an informal language which is readily understood by their peers. In the very act of explaining or attempting to explain an idea, the student must reach for a deeper understanding of that idea. As students work together, they begin to recognize the need for more precise language to express their ideas. Once they have achieved deeper understanding and clarity, students are ready to adopt the more formal language of mathematical discourse that is used by their instructors and the authors of their textbooks.

Mathematics offers many opportunities for exploring open-ended and non-routine problem situations. Students can make conjectures, pose problems, and work together toward problem solutions. Students seem to feel free to ask questions of their peers in small groups, even when they are reluctant to ask questions of the instructor, especially during whole-class discussion. Mathematics problems are particularly well suited for group discussion because they have solutions that can be logically demonstrated. Moreover, when students are working with peers, they are more likely to see alternative approaches than when they are watching their instructor demonstrate a solution. Since they recognize the instructor as an authority in the field, they are less likely to question her approach. When several students are working together, they may solve a problem using two or more very different approaches. Thus, they verify the solution while also learning that there are several correct ways to approach the problem. Working together, students can help one another master basic skills, and they learn to apply these skills in the context of meaningful and challenging problems. Finally, students working together in small groups can tackle problems that are somewhat beyond the competence of each as individuals at their particular developmental levels.

Small group learning offers opportunities for all students to take an active part in meaningful and complementary ways. Each student has a variety of skills to bring to group work. Some students are quick with basic computations, some grasp new concepts easily; some students work very easily with calculators and computers, while others have good reading skills. Some students have a hard time getting started with a problem, yet they can often complete a solution once they get started; others are very good at taking the first step. Some students are very quick and usually right, and thus they have difficulty checking their own work. Sometimes the slow plodding student who keeps asking "How did you get this result?" helps to uncover errors in the quicker student's solutions.

In a well-functioning cooperative learning group, students learn to recognize and draw on each other's skills. It is important that the instructor pay attention to how groups are functioning and encourage all students to continue to engage in learning. We say more about this in later chapters.

The National Council of Teachers of Mathematics (1989, 2000) has suggested the use of small groups in conjunction with other instructional methods in mathematics to help accomplish its major curriculum standards: mathematics as problem solving, mathematics as reasoning, mathematics as communication, and making mathematical connections. The Mathematical Association of America has published many works dealing with reform in the teaching of mathematics. Many of the curriculum reform projects supported by the National Science Foundation in response to the call for a "lean and lively" calculus employ some form of cooperative learning in small groups. For example, eight of the ten reports on such curriculum reform projects which are included in *Priming the Calculus Pump* (Tucker, 1990) explicitly mention the use of small groups of students working together as integral to the project; and almost a third of the 68 abstracts of projects included in this volume also mention small group work.

Many Ways to Use Cooperative Learning in Mathematics

There are many ways that cooperative learning activities can be used in mathematics classes to introduce new concepts, to review and reinforce skills, and to bring together and synthesize ideas that the students have been studying. Chapter 3 presents and discusses a variety of classroom strategies that the authors have used in their own classrooms. The instructor might ask students to discuss certain problems in pairs or in small groups. Alternatively, the students might be directed to check their homework with each other and to identify those problems that need further clarification or input.

One of the authors has used a textbook that has a set of true/false review questions at the end of each reading assignment. As a standing assignment, the students are to come to class prepared to support their true/false responses with specific references to the text. When they first come to class, groups of four students compare their responses, and the groups present for class discussion those items that they are unable to resolve in the small-group discussion. On occasions when the students are still unable to resolve the problem after some whole-class discussion, this instructor often has the students re-read the selection for the next class period, and she again asks the students to be prepared to support their responses with reference to the text. In this way, the small- and large-group discussions help the students learn to read their text more carefully.

In small classes with enough board space, students can be asked to work together in their groups using panels of the blackboard. The boardwork provides a common focus for group discussion and problem solving. The instructor easily scans the entire room, gauges the progress of the groups, and offers suggestions as needed.

While a carefully prepared lecture is effective in introducing students to a particular way of solving a certain problem, group discussion often engages the students in creative thinking and brainstorming so that the students see multiple perspectives and approaches to solving the same problem. This gives students experience in developing problem solutions, which is a distinctly different skill from that of applying a strategy they have observed the instructor demonstrate.

Problems might be posed for students working in groups. Some textbooks include guided-inquiry tasks that facilitate small-group discussion of concepts before these concepts are presented formally through the reading assignments or short lectures. Working on these problems offers the students opportunities to explore and investigate particular mathematical situations, to make and test conjectures, and even to prove theorems.

Many of the authors introduce new concepts to the class through group work on problems that include technology-based tasks. The students may be asked to construct a computer function that models the situation presented in a word problem or to investigate a particular function or family of functions using a graphing calculator or computer graphing software. Students might be asked to draw, measure, or construct something with particular attributes. In high school geometry, some of us remember being asked to perform certain constructions in Euclidean geometry using a compass and straightedge; geometry software is now available that makes it possible for our students to do similar constructions in the hyperbolic plane.

Many of us have had the experience of coming to understand an idea only when we have tried to teach it to someone else. Peer tutoring is one way of giving students an opportunity to do some of this teaching themselves. Students might be asked to explain or review an idea or concept or to demonstrate how they have done a particular calculation. Some of the authors have found it to be enlightening to listen in on some of the conversations that our students have during such in-class tutoring sessions. As the students try to explain something to each other, they have to find words to express the idea. This very process of articulating an idea facilitates and reinforces the student's own understanding of the material.

Quizzes, tests, and exams are a fact of life in the collegiate classroom. Small groups can work together to review material at the end of a chapter or to prepare for a test. The students might be directed to solve particular problems, perhaps chosen from the review questions at the end of the chapter or unit, and then to check each other's work on these problems. Students might make up their own questions for each other and then check their work on these problems. Some of the authors have experimented with using some group quizzes and an occasional group test, and they have found that group testing can be very effective. Group testing is discussed more fully in Chapter 4.

Theoretical Distinctions in the Field of Small-Group Learning

The foundational concepts for cooperative learning have their roots in social or educational psychology and in educational sociology, whereas collaborative learning is based in psycholinguistics and constructivist philosophy. These parallel traditions emerged separately from different philosophical bases. Their proponents have attended different professional conferences and have published in different settings. In general, the cooperative learning approaches tend to be more highly structured, with more focus on cooperative behaviors and, in some approaches, the use of rewards. Those of the collaborative learning tradition, *e.g.*, Britton (1970), tend not to micro-manage group activities, not to break tasks into small component parts, and not to provide rewards

In the cooperative learning tradition, groups tend to be organized and structured with active teacher facilitation. In some cooperative learning procedures, instructors explicitly teach students interpersonal skills such as including everyone, listening with respect, using people's names, and disagreeing in an agreeable manner. In the collaborative learning tradition, groups tend to be more loosely organized and unstructured, with relatively little teacher facilitation; instructors generally believe that college and university students are adults who already have the skills to conduct effective small-group discussions. See Matthews, Cooper, Davidson, and Hawkes (1995).

In some cooperative learning models, there is discussion of task and maintenance functions for the group members. Examples of task functions include proposing an idea, clarifying, summarizing, recording, and reporting results to the whole class. Examples of group maintenance functions are including everyone, inviting contributions from others, praising or encouraging, and showing respect for minority views. In some cooperative models, these functions are assigned as roles that rotate among the group members. These ideas are examined more fully in Chapter 2.

It is difficult to draw a hard and fast distinction between cooperative and collaborative learning, and the differences in orientation can be viewed as a source of strength because the perspectives are mutually enriching. Actually, there are more similarities than differences when we compare cooperative and collaborative approaches. The most widely known approaches to cooperative or collaborative small-group learning are Student Team Learning (Slavin, 1983; 1989/90), Learning Together (Johnson and R. Johnson, 1987; 1989a, b), Group Investigation (Sharan and Hertz-Lazarowitz, 1982; Sharan and Sharan, 1992), the Structural Approach (Kagan, 1992), Complex Instruction (Cohen, 1986, 1994), and the Collaborative Approach (Barnes, Britton, and Torbe, 1986; Britton, 1970; Brubacher, Payne, and Rickett, 1990; Reid, Forrestal, and Cook, 1989; and Bruffee, 1993). Most of the cited approaches are summarized in a handbook by Sharan (1993) and in a theoretical synthesis paper that offers a conceptual framework for comparing and contrasting the approaches to cooperative and collaborative learning (Davidson, 1994). In that synthesis we find five attributes that are common to all and that could therefore be considered critical attributes of cooperative and collaborative learning. These attributes are:

1. a common task or learning activity suitable for group work;
2. small-group interaction focused on the learning activity;
3. cooperative, mutually helpful behavior among students;

4. interdependence in working together; and
5. individual accountability and responsibility.

Beyond these critical attributes are a number of points that different theorists employ in varying ways, if at all, and that, therefore, cannot be considered critical attributes of cooperative or collaborative learning. Several of these attributes have caused continuing ideological debate among different schools of thought. We briefly mention some of these points here.

There is considerable discussion (and no clear consensus) on grouping procedures. Should the groups be formed of students based on heterogeneous or homogeneous attributes? For instance, should the students have similar academic strengths or backgrounds? Should students be put in groups based on achievement scores or grades in previous courses? Should the teacher attempt to put students into groups based on certain criteria, or should the groups be assigned randomly? Should students self-select their groups or have some input into the group formation process? Should collegiate-level groups be based on some common interest, for instance, a student's major?

Many theorists are strong proponents of structuring positive interdependence among the group members, *e.g.,* via goals, tasks, resource interdependence, assigned or structured roles, division of labor, or rewards. Some favor the explicit teaching of interpersonal, relationship, cooperative, or collaborative skills.

In some models of cooperative/collaborative learning, emphasis is given to reflection (or processing) on social skills, academic skills, or group dynamics. Some models include climate-setting through class-building, team-building, trust-building activities, or through the development of cooperative norms. We say more about this in Chapter 2.

Some proponents of cooperative learning have given considerable attention to problems of social status. In some settings, certain students are seen by their peers as being more attractive (or better) by virtue of such attributes as race, ethnic background, gender, or even family connections. Some models of cooperative learning favor teacher behaviors that tend to increase the status of low-status students, for example, by identifying or highlighting competencies of low-status students and focusing peers' attention on those competencies (Cohen, 1994).

In discussions of cooperative/collaborative learning, attention is given to group structure, and to organizing the communication patterns within the group. In some models, group leadership responsibilities are shared through formal structures or roles and rotated among the students; in other models, these are not designated. Some theorists place more importance on the role of the teacher in different phases of the lesson. Some put an emphasis on equal participation by all students and/or on simultaneous interaction among students in pairs or small groups. (See various works by Spencer Kagan.)

Proponents of active learning through small-group interaction have much in common with one another, even though they may use different strategies or techniques in implementing cooperative or collaborative strategies in their classrooms. It seems useful to emphasize the attributes common to all cooperative and collaborative approaches. Then teachers who are implementing small-group and cooperative learning strategies in their own teaching can make careful selections among the various approaches, and they can adapt additional attributes that fit their own personal philosophies, instructional and curricular goals, and classroom settings. The fact that many curriculum projects employ informal groupwork, rather than specific cooperative models, leaves teachers free to make their own informed decisions about how to implement cooperative groups. This can work, provided that teachers have access to suitable professional development for cooperative or collaborative learning, to enable them to organize and facilitate effective groupwork from whatever perspective they have chosen. Many of us have observed that reading the literature about cooperative and collaborative learning is helpful, but doing so does not make any instructor a skilled implementor of these methods. Attending faculty development seminars or workshops on cooperative/collaborative learning (such as the MAA Project CLUME Workshops) can make a great difference in implementing these models effectively. It also helps to understand that changing instructional practice is a long-term process, not a quick event. See Brody and Davidson (1998).

The following chart contrasts the role of teachers in cooperative and collaborative learning.

In Cooperative Learning, teachers are more likely to:	In Collaborative Learning, teachers are more likely to:
Consider a variety of procedures for forming groups.	Let students form their own groups.
Provide structure for the communication pattern within groups, or assign roles.	Let groups interact as they see fit, and select their own roles (if any).
Monitor the mathematical task performance of the groups and provide assistance as needed through hints, questions, etc.	Let the group proceed independently on the task, and offer assistance only on request.
Teach cooperative skills (social skills, communication skills) if/when needed.	Assume that students know how to work together in groups.
Help students resolve communication problems in groups.	Assume that students can resolve communication problems.
Employ classroom management techniques such as timed activities, quiet signal, structured room arrangement, assigned and rotating roles.	Leave the room occasionally to foster student independence, and let students make decisions about room arrangement and timing.

Research Base

Cooperative learning has been among the most widely investigated approaches in the educational research literature. Hundreds of studies have compared the effects of cooperative learning with other instructional methods such as the lecture method or individualized instruction. For syntheses of this research, see extensive reviews by Johnson and Johnson (1989a), Slavin (1990), Sharan (1980, 1990), and Newmann and Thompson (1987). Research conducted in many different subject areas and various age groups of students has generally shown positive effects favoring cooperative learning in the areas of academic achievement, development of higher order thinking, self-esteem and self-confidence as learners, intergroup relations including friendships across racial and ethnic boundaries, social acceptance of mainstreamed students labeled as handicapped or disabled, development of social skills, and the ability to take the perspective of another person. These results apply also in the learning of mathematics. See a review by Davidson (1985) and an overview of research by Davidson and Kroll (1991). While achievement comparisons between cooperative classes and lecture classes sometimes show a tie (that is, no significant difference), it is extremely rare to find a case with higher outcomes for the lecture classes. Differences, when they exist, are almost always in favor of the cooperative classes. A recent meta-analysis (Springer, Stanne, and Donovan, 1999) of research with post-secondary students in science, mathematics, engineering, and technology shows significant, positive main effects of cooperative learning upon achievement, persistence, and attitudes among undergraduates. Another line of research has focused on interactions in cooperative groups. Webb (1991) has analyzed research in mathematics that linked task-related verbal interaction to learning in small groups, and she has also examined the effects of various compositions of groups, *e.g.*, mixed-ability or uniform-ability groups. A review by Cohen (1994) focuses on conditions under which small groups are most productive, including research on the relationship of small-group interaction to outcomes and the kinds of communication that lead to varied learning outcomes. A volume edited by Hertz-Lazarowitz and Miller (1992) integrates related research from the fields of education, developmental psychology, and social psychology in an examination of the dynamics of group processes, interaction, and outcomes.

Large-Scale Implementations of Cooperative Learning in Mathematics

The field of cooperative learning in mathematics has advanced considerably since its early development in the late 1960s. There are now several examples of large-scale implementations in undergraduate mathematics. By this we mean colleges or universities engaged in cooperative learning with multiple courses, or multiple sections, or multiple instructors, or multiple teaching assistants (whom we hope have had some training). These larger-scale implementations include both large

universities and smaller private liberal arts colleges. We offer here short descriptions of what is being done at a few colleges and universities with no attempt to be exhaustive. The method of selection for this short sampling was done in a highly biased non-scientific way by contacting individuals with whom some of the authors have had personal or professional contacts. The purpose of these descriptions is to show a range of practical ways to implement cooperative learning in collegiate mathematics in a wide variety of settings.

The Honors Workshop Model

In the early 1990s, Uri Treisman did a comparative study of Black and Chinese calculus students at Berkeley. While Black students had high motivation, strong family support, and excellent high school preparation, and while they spent much time studying alone, they were failing calculus at a higher rate than other students. The Chinese students as a group, on the other hand, had the lowest failure rate among the university's first-year calculus students. The significant difference that Treisman found between these two groups lay not in their level of income, motivation, academic preparation, or family support, but in the way they studied. The Black students tended to do most of their studying alone, while the Chinese students did private study in preparation for participation in collaborative study sessions (or "study gangs"). Building on insights gained through this study, Treisman developed an Honors Workshop model for minority students in first-year calculus at Berkeley that has been successfully replicated on many campuses (Treisman, 1992). Black students who participated in this model at Berkeley experienced major gains in academic achievement and success in mathematics.

University of Maryland, College Park, Maryland

Extensive use of small groups in learning mathematics at the University of Maryland has a history dating back more than thirty years. Davidson's work in calculus began in 1968 and was followed by development of an abstract algebra course (Davidson and Gulick, 1976a) and a linear algebra course by Jerome Dancis. A multi-section course in mathematics for prospective elementary teachers was created by Mildred Cole *et al.* (University of Maryland Mathematics Project, 1978).

Close-Contact Calculus at the University of Maryland grew out of an effort by Scott Wolpert and Denny Gulick to adapt the Treisman method to serve large numbers of students at a large public university. Students working in small groups focused their attention on worksheets that had multi-step problems with mixture of the algebraic, graphical, numerical, and narrative approaches. These classes had a substantially reduced attrition, and they routinely out-performed other sections of the calculus course.

In 1994 Close-Contact Calculus tailored this method to reach all students taking first-year calculus. Each class of approximately 200 students meets three times per week in large lecture sessions. For two other meetings, there are discussion sessions of about 20 students, who work together in small groups of four to five students. For the first third of the discussion session, students work together to finish homework problems. The rest of the time the students solve problems on worksheets prepared especially for the course. The Teaching Assistants act as facilitators who generally "answer questions" by asking pertinent and leading questions. The professor occasionally visits the sections. Both the worksheets and the homework are graded, and there is an effort to give frequent feedback to the students about their progress.

The goals of the Close-Contact Calculus at the University of Maryland have been:

- To reduce attrition in class registration from drop-add day to the end of the semester; generally this goal has been accomplished.
- To increase students' satisfaction with the course and to improve their perception of calculus, independent of their performance on tests and final examination; for a large majority of the students, this has been accomplished.
- To help students develop a better understanding of calculus and to improve performance on tests and the final examination; there is a marginal increase in understanding; however, the fact that students work together on problems seems to detract from their ability to solve problems individually on tests.

On the whole, the University of Maryland has been pleased with the Close-Contact Calculus. However, as with any teaching method, continuing evaluation and adjustments are crucial to its continued effectiveness.

University of Michigan, Ann Arbor, Michigan

The Michigan Calculus Project is the mainline program for first-year calculus, which is taken by approximately 5000 students each year at the University of Michigan. Classes, which meet three times per week for 90-minute sessions, are kept to a maximum of 32 students. Students sit at tables and work cooperatively in the classroom. Each classroom has an overhead projector for instructor or student presentations. This course emphasizes oral and written communication of mathematics as well as the development of in-depth understanding of specific mathematical concepts. Students are expected to read the textbook and to participate in team homework assignments, which consist of challenging problems that require reasoning and interpretation. Team homework, which is regularly assigned and graded by the instructor, counts about 25% of the final grade.

A one-week instructor training program for new instructors (including senior faculty who are teaching in this program for the first time) precedes the fall term. There are usually about 50 new instructors each fall. This training program is a workshop on classroom cooperative learning techniques using problems from the text as examples, and it includes an introduction to the philosophy and goals of the course, the course syllabus, and the use of technology with cooperative learning.

To provide support throughout the semester, the course leaders send instructors suggested activities and teaching tips for each class day. Trainers visit each new instructor's class twice in the first term, and they conduct a mid-semester assessment that involves both classroom observations and a discussion with students (without the instructor present) about the strengths of the course and recommendations for change. Following this assessment, the observer writes a confidential report for the instructor and meets with the instructor to give feedback.

Piedmont College, Demorest, Georgia

Piedmont College, a private college in northern Georgia, uses cooperative learning extensively in its undergraduate mathematics courses and exclusively in the content courses leading to the Master of Arts in Teaching degree. The department is composed of four full-time faculty and several adjunct faculty. One department member, Betty Rogers, has been associated with the Mathematical Association of America's Project CLUME workshops since 1995, and another faculty member has co-authored a statistics text for cooperative classes (Rossman and von Oehsen, 1997). Although approaches to cooperative learning vary among the department members and adjuncts, most instructors lean toward implementation of the ACE-cycle (Activities, Class discussion, Exercises), which is discussed in Chapter 6.

Every faculty member has expressed satisfaction with the cooperative approach, and one professor who recently initiated cooperative strategies states that he wishes he had begun cooperative classes earlier. Student feedback indicates that they enjoy cooperative learning, and some students express the feeling that they might not have been as successful in certain courses if the class had been taught by traditional lecture. This strategy has been particularly successful in four-hour evening classes with non-traditional students.

Approximately fifty percent of the mathematics majors become secondary mathematics teachers. These students say that participation in cooperative classes is one of the major benefits of their Piedmont College experience.

Cardinal Stritch University, Milwaukee, Wisconsin

At Cardinal Stritch University every member of the Department of Mathematics and Computer Science uses some form of cooperative learning in her classes. The department is relatively small with four full-time and approximately six part-time faculty. Reynolds is co-leader of MAA Project CLUME, and two other faculty members have participated in Project CLUME. Unofficially auditing each other's courses provides semester-long opportunities for observing and critiquing each other's implementations of cooperative learning strategies. Each of these instructors uses cooperative learning in somewhat different ways. There is considerable discussion among both faculty and students about cooperative strategies.

The experience at Stritch shows that it is possible to implement cooperative learning both inside and outside class in a commuter school with many non-traditional students. Although the student body consists mainly of commuters and about half of the students are over the age of 25 with jobs and family responsibilities, they expect to work in small groups in one way or another in every course. Graduates of this department have reported that the interpersonal skills they learned informally through participation in cooperative learning groups have been important in their workplace settings in both education and business/industry.

Ursinus College, Collegeville, Pennsylvania

A similar use of cooperative learning has developed in the Mathematics and Computer Science Department at Ursinus College, a coeducational residential liberal arts college near Philadelphia, Pennsylvania. The seven full-time and one part-time member all have incorporated aspects of cooperative learning in their mathematics and computer science courses. The initial use of cooperative learning in the department was part of a calculus reform effort, and gradually cooperative learning was adopted in other courses. Currently two professors use cooperative learning, as defined earlier in this chapter, in all their courses. Other instructors have their students work in groups at various times and in various ways. Students work together during scheduled computer laboratory periods, out of class on projects and preparation of group oral presentations, and during class on activities such as data collection and analysis in elementary statistics classes.

In recent discussions, the six faculty members who taught at Ursinus before cooperative learning was introduced noted the marked change in attitude toward student collaboration. Previously, these professors envisioned students learning while solving problems alone with little interaction; in some courses there were penalties for any evidence of collusion on homework and projects. Now students are encouraged to work together even in courses where they submit individual work. There is general recognition by both students and faculty members that learning is greatly advanced during the hours that students spend studying and working on problems in their groups.

Georgia State University, Atlanta, Georgia

Two faculty members including Ed Dubinsky, co-leader of Project CLUME, and three graduate students who have been trained in the use of cooperative learning utilize this pedagogical strategy in all of their classes at Georgia State. Since 1996 a reform calculus program (Calculus, Concepts, Computers and Cooperative Learning, sometimes referred to as "C4L Calculus") has been offered at Georgia State. Usually four sections of calculus are offered per term with a total enrollment of 100–120 students. The sections are coordinated with common assignments and examinations. Students in each section work in fixed groups for the term. All homework and some examinations are completed as group assignments.

In addition, courses such as Discrete Mathematics, Abstract Algebra, College Algebra, Mathematics for Elementary Education majors, Statistics, Business Calculus and Mathematics for Liberal Arts have been taught in this manner.

Purdue University North Central, Westville, Indiana

At Purdue University North Central (PUNC), a regional campus in the Purdue University Statewide System, almost all full-time (and many part-time) faculty members of the Mathematics/Physics Department use some form of cooperative learning in their classes. PUNC offers mostly courses in the first two years of college mathematics, statistics, and physics, and the department offers some upper-level classes in these disciplines. The department consists of eight full-time faculty: four mathematicians, one statistician, and three physicists. Several members of the faculty have attended the NSF-supported Calculus, Concepts, Computers and Cooperative Learning (C4L Calculus) workshops offered through Purdue University from 1991–1996.

Cooperative learning was first used in calculus classes at PUNC. Then it spread to physics classes, the developmental and college algebra, trigonometry, and statistics classes. The mathematics courses for elementary education majors are taught using a constructivist perspective on learning and cooperative learning groups. The first-year engineering and physics classes and the four-semester calculus sequence for engineering, science and mathematics students all use a fully integrated computer laboratory component. All statistics classes use either a fully integrated computer lab or calculator lab component.

Each faculty member uses cooperative

learning in somewhat different ways and there is considerable discussion among both faculty and students about cooperative learning strategies. A peer collaboration program involving all faculty in small groups (with the groups changed each semester or year) includes the unofficial auditing of each other's classes and informal meetings for the exchange of cooperative learning experiences and implementation strategies. This process provides continuing opportunities for observing and critiquing each other's uses of cooperative learning strategies.

PUNC students regularly report that the interpersonal skills they learned informally through participation in cooperative learning groups have been important in their workplace settings and in many of their other class experiences.

Agder College, Kristiansand, Norway

At Agder College in Norway a form of small group teaching has been used since 1973. Typically 50–300 students attend lectures and need additional instruction in problem solving. In applied subjects such as statistics and economics, the solution to a problem may be less interesting than the model underlying the solution. Small groups are ideally suited to discuss such models.

Agder College has more than 50 rooms equipped for small-group learning. These rooms are made available for student use during scheduled two-hour periods. Students are given exercises for group work during these sessions, but they are not evaluated on these exercises. Most of the problems are taken from textbooks. Small projects that can be completed by a group in less than two hours may also be assigned. One or more teachers circulate among the groups to provide assistance as needed.

Attendance is not compulsory, and the students are given the responsibility for forming the groups themselves. The small group sessions make a major difference for average and below-average students. The better students seem to manage well without attending groups. However, most of the stronger students participate, not so much because they need the groups to pass the examination, but because group work is enjoyable, and because two hours spent in a well-functioning group may save many lonely hours of work.

This system is used in a majority of the courses. During fall, 1993, there were 715 small groups, each having an average number of about six students. In the larger courses, Basic Mathematics and Basic Statistics, there are presently about 300 students and 50 groups.

Looking Back . . . and Ahead . . .

If, as is often said, experience is the mother of wisdom, this volume offers the collective wisdom of the 17 authors of the following chapters. We share here our experiences in implementing cooperative learning in our own classes, and our reflections on those experiences. We have attempted to use cooperative learning in ways that fit our different institutional settings and our different personalities and temperaments. Sometimes things we tried didn't work quite as expected. (Sometimes it didn't work as well as we had hoped; sometimes it worked in ways that exceeded our expectations.) We have reflected on what we had attempted and on what we saw occurring in our classes. We have learned much from what we have tried, and we have learned much more in sharing our experiences with each other. We have listened to each other and to our colleagues, many of whom have participated in MAA Project CLUME summer workshops held from 1995 through 1999. In the remaining chapters of this book, we offer our present understanding of what has worked in our own classes and why we think it works. If you ask us again in another couple of years about cooperative learning in undergraduate mathematics, we will probably have tried some new strategies, gathered some additional ideas, and reflected some more on what we are learning. We may, then, have an even better understanding of how cooperative learning works. In this volume we offer our current understandings.

Chapter 2

Practical Implementation Issues within the Individual Classroom

Nancy L. Hagelgans, William E. Fenton, Bernadette M. Baker, Clare Hemenway

Introduction

In this chapter we begin our discussion of practical issues with the use of various physical layouts of classrooms and computer laboratories in a cooperative learning setting. Then we describe specific ways to orient the students to cooperative learning at the start of a course. Finally, we address the student groups: setting the duration of the groups, choosing the size of the groups, arranging the students in groups, and maintaining productive groups. We share our own experiences and the experiences of the respondents to the CLUME Survey with the hope that these experiences will guide other instructors as they make decisions that affect students in cooperative learning groups throughout a course in their own classrooms.

Classrooms and Computer Laboratories

Physical Layouts: Classrooms

Instructors face a variety of classrooms, and these classrooms may either help or hinder their efforts to implement cooperative learning. Although instructors usually do not design the classrooms in which they teach, they may be able to request particular rooms or work for changes that will help their class time to be more productive. Instructors can make minor adjustments in the rooms to facilitate learning, and they can overcome some difficulties with their classrooms.

In a class where the students sit in their cooperative learning groups, the most important consideration is space. The students need space to see the work of the other students in their group, and they need space to take notes and to work individually. Students should have a clear view of the chalkboard from their groups' locations. There should be enough space between the student groups so that the instructor can move comfortably around the room to interact with each group. There should be extensive chalkboard space, especially if student groups are to work simultaneously at the chalkboard. And, if the course involves graphing calculators or other technology, a projection screen that does not cover the usable chalkboard space should be available.

Cooperative learning is noisy! Even if the room is crowded, students need to hear each other in their group work and in discussions with the entire class. There is little that instructors can do to change the acoustics of an overly "live" room. When an instructor wants to get the students' attention, he can use a signal, such as flicking the lights or rapping on the chalkboard. One surprisingly effective method is to raise a hand and wait.

Three common classroom settings are: classrooms with tables and chairs, rooms with movable desk chairs, and lecture halls with fixed chairs. With some forethought, an instructor can use any of these classrooms effectively with cooperative learning groups.

The classroom with small tables and chairs is well suited to cooperative learning in mathematics courses.

Students in a group sit at a table, where they can face each other, share materials readily, and work together comfortably. The width of a rectangular table and the diameter of a circular table should not be so large that conversation across the table is difficult. Very small tables can be pushed together to create a common work area for a group. The instructor should arrange the furniture or give specific directions to students at first, but students soon learn to rearrange the furniture in ways suitable to the current activity.

During discussions in class students turn their chairs to face the front of the room, the instructor, the chalkboard, or the projection screen. The atmosphere of a very small class acting as a single group is very different when all the students and the instructor sit at one table.

In a classroom with individual desk chairs, the chairs can be moved into clusters of three or four chairs.

The members of one group of at most four students make a common work area from their individual desks. Students in a group with five or more members must move their desk tops as close as possible to avoid separating into subgroups. The instructor should plan the clusters so that there is separation between the groups. Any extra desk chairs that inhibit his or her walking among the groups can be moved aside. As in a classroom with tables and chairs, the instructor should either arrange the furniture or give specific directions to students for the first few class meetings. Students adjust their own chairs during the class hour as they change between working together and looking toward the front of the room.

The lecture hall poses special challenges.

Students seated in fixed chairs have difficulty facing the other members of their groups, and the instructor finds that moving throughout the room is awkward. However, whenever space permits, the students can be seated in ways that promote cooperative learning. For example, students in groups of size four can follow the seating pattern indicated in the diagram below, where "S" represents a seated student and "e" represents an empty seat:

S S e S S e S S e...

S S e S S e S S e...

e e e e e e e e e...

S S e S S e S S e...

S S e S S e S S e...

e e e e e e e e e...

The instructor sees each group clearly and uses the empty rows to circulate among the groups. The front students in a group turn to face their other group members, who are seated behind them. In a large auditorium, the groups can be encouraged (perhaps by a few extra-credit points) to show large signs with the group's name or the students' names.

Physical Layouts: Computer Laboratories

Many of the concerns for cooperative learning in classrooms apply also to cooperative learning in a computer laboratory. However, computer laboratories tend to be less flexible than regular classrooms since a laboratory's configuration is usually fixed. Whenever instructors can alter the layout or specify the arrangement in a new facility, they can develop a laboratory conducive to cooperative learning. Those planning laboratories for mathematics classes should remember that the computer is merely another tool and not the main focus of the students' activities. The arrangement of the facility should discourage the natural student attitude that the computer is the primary object in the room.

As in a classroom, the computer laboratory should support different modes of student interaction, including large-group, small-group, and individual work, as well as easy transitions between different modes. In particular, the students need room to work comfortably alone or in groups, and with or without

14

Practical Implementation Issues

the computers. There should be adequate space for texts, papers, and notebooks. Students should be able to face each other when they are working together in their groups. The design of many computer labs with rows of computers all facing the same direction inhibits group work for groups of more than two or three students, and barriers between computers may separate students from their group members. The monitors should be large enough so that all members of a group can simultaneously view one monitor, and students should be able to turn off the monitors, or the computers, to avoid distraction when computers are not in use. Comfortable chairs help students through longer sessions, and chairs with wheels allow students to move freely between nearby computers as they change between individual and group work.

The computer lab should be arranged so that the instructor can easily circulate among the student groups and view the monitors while the students are seated in their chairs. One or more aisles, especially in a lab with rows of computers, may improve the layout so that the instructor's access to all the computers is possible during a laboratory session.

Students should have an unobstructed view of the instructor and any presentations from their seats in the laboratory, and the instructor should be able to make eye contact with all the students during any discussions with the whole class. Whiteboards and projection screens usually can be raised so that the monitors do not block the students' view. Some laboratories have monitors mounted on pivot arms so that the monitors can be moved out of the line of sight. Others have monitors located beneath glass tops with movable shields to cut glare. Computer tables can be placed on raised tiers to improve visibility for both the instructor and the students.

Many laboratory configurations have been tried. We will describe several configurations that have been used successfully for cooperative learning groups of students.

1. The computers are arranged in a "horseshoe" along three walls of the room with another "horseshoe" of empty tables inside the first horseshoe. Whiteboards and screens are placed along the fourth wall. In a very large laboratory, additional horseshoes can be nested within the horseshoe adjacent to the walls. Students readily turn their chairs, especially if the chairs are swivel chairs, from the computers to the empty tables in the inner horseshoe for paper and pencil work. Variations of this configuration replace the inner

horseshoe of empty tables with both tables and chairs or desk chairs in the room's interior to which students move as needed. In the diagram below, each "c" indicates a computer in the horseshoe of computers and each "t" represents part of the horseshoe of tables.

2. The computers are mounted on small tables that are placed back-to-back around the room. This arrangement requires any electric and network plugs needed to be available in the floor at appropriate locations throughout the laboratory. The tables can be arranged to avoid long rows and to create space for the instructor to circulate. Flexible arrangements that fit the groups in each laboratory session are possible if the tables have wheels. In the diagram below "TT" represents two small tables with one computer on each table.

3. Two computers are mounted facing inward on the short ends of each rectangular table, and two chairs are placed on each of the other sides of the table. The students have the open space in the middle of the table for work. All students in a group of four can see both monitors on their table. The rectangle below represents one such table; each "C" represents a computer on the table.

4.   The computers are arranged in various ways throughout the room. Some computers on long tables face two walls; this arrangement generally works well for groups of three students or for students working in pairs. Some rectangular tables are placed with a shorter end against one of the other walls, and four computers are placed along the other three sides of each of these tables. The whiteboard is on one wall with these tables and can be accessed only between the tables. After some guidance from the instructor, student groups have the freedom to choose a way to sit together in a way compatible with the number of students in the group and with the particular mode of working at the time. In the diagram below, each "C" represents a computer placed on the table against the wall, and each "TTTTT" represents a rectangular table with four computers.

```
    C  C   C   C   C   C   C
 TTTTT                   TTTTT
 TTTTT                   TTTTT
 TTTTT                   TTTTT
    C  C   C   C   C   C   C
```

These four laboratory arrangements allow students to work comfortably within their groups and, by turning their chairs, to participate in any activities of the entire class.

Student Orientation to Cooperative Learning

The first few days of a course are crucial times for establishing the student attitudes and expectations for the semester. Students' early experiences with group activities in a course largely determine the social and academic climate for the ensuing weeks. An effective orientation to cooperative learning includes many aspects of orientation programs for new college students: introduction through student participation to people, facilities, social rules, and academic expectations. Community-building group activities may be purely social in nature, or they may involve mathematical activities appropriate for the students. Many instructors use several different types of activities, and respondents to the CLUME Survey reported that they used a regular mathematical assignment done in groups more frequently than all the other methods combined. The primary aim of the orientation activities is to convince the students of the pleasure and value of cooperative learning, especially if their previous experience has been in competitive classes or in classes where they were expected to work alone to complete assignments and to learn the material.

The initial activity may be used to introduce the students to each other. In one such introductory activity, as students sign in on the chalkboard, a sheet of paper, or their computer screens, they introduce themselves to the class, or the instructor asks each student the same question or a different question. Such questions may be related to mathematics, *e.g.,* the students are asked what they liked best about the last mathematics course that they took, or each student is asked to give a different fact or formula from a previous mathematics course. Advanced students may briefly describe any summer work or internships with emphasis on how they used their academic background. In large classes, or when a more intimate approach is wanted, pairs of students interview each other, and then each student introduces the other member of the pair to a larger group or to the entire class.

An instant survey is one method that uncovers similarities and differences among the students, and it promotes the idea that students are not tied to their seats. All the students stand at the front of the room, and they separate into groups at designated areas of the room according to their answers. Questions may include nonmathematical preferences, such as whether or not the students like country music. The instructor asks several questions in rapid succession, and some questions may be solicited from the students. In a variation of the instant survey, groups of four to five students find characteristics or preferences shared by all or a specified number of students in the group. In another approach, each student lists five of his or her characteristics (such as major, commuter or not, type of music preferred), some of which may be specified by the instructor. Then the students circulate in the room to find other students who share most of these attributes, or those students who are most different.

Practical Implementation Issues

Even the syllabus can be used to facilitate interaction and participation. For example, in one method used before the entire class goes over the syllabus, the instructor hands out numbered questions, some humorous and some serious, to a few students as they enter the classroom. The students participate as they ask their prepared questions at the appropriate time in the discussion of the syllabus. An alternative method has student pairs reading and explaining syllabus sections to each other before an opportunity to ask their questions of the instructor.

The introductory strategies described above work well to introduce students to each other in both traditional lecture courses and in courses where cooperative learning is the major pedagogical strategy. However, many instructors who use cooperative learning prefer to involve groups of students immediately in solving mathematical problems.

The development of productive group behavior requires practice and guidance. Ideally members of a group learn to provide mutual support, exchange ideas, share resources, coach each other, and celebrate successes. The goal is to develop a sense of interdependence, a belief that together everyone accomplishes and learns more. To benefit fully from group work, the group must learn to work as a group, not as a collection of individuals.

Once students know each other, some class time should be spent discussing the value of cooperative learning as well as group operations and expectations. Since doing mathematics cooperatively is a new experience for many students, there may be both passive and active resistance if students are not properly prepared for this approach. In addition, some students may resent any form of group work because they have had bad experiences in project groups with group members who contributed little to the work.

From the outset, the instructor should ensure that students understand that group work is a mandatory, integral component of the course. Some students respond favorably to an explanation of the expected benefits of group work, namely improved learning of mathematics and preparation for team work in the workplace. Most students respond to clear statements of how the group work will affect their grade in the course. This effect should be substantial enough that students take the group work seriously. On the other hand, each instructor should consider the delicate balance between encouraging group work and inflating course grades. (We discuss grading in greater depth in Chapter 4.)

Some class time near the beginning of the course should be devoted to discussing issues related to cooperative learning. Such discussions can influence students before they have acquired a set way of operating in their groups. The students sit either in their temporary groups or in their permanent groups as they address the following topics: desirable characteristics of students in a group, specific tasks or roles that group members need to perform, behaviors that could hinder effective group work, behaviors that could lead to effective group work, and different ways that a group can approach an assignment. After the student groups discuss each topic, the instructor writes the groups' responses on the chalkboard. The instructor can supplement the responses to ensure that his or her expectations are included. As students discuss these questions and hear the responses of others, they realize that very specific elements are needed to effectively complete work with the members of their groups. In addition, they experience the way that much class time may be spent throughout the course. Some instructors ask the students to address such issues in their journals before the class discussion so those students think about them several times.

How might students respond in these discussions? In the experience of the authors, the following lists usually are constructed.

The characteristics of an effective group include:

- organizational skills,
- conflict resolution,
- expertise with any technology required,
- writing skills,
- mathematics skills,
- and common times to meet outside of class.

The tasks and roles that individual group members assume are:

- manager,
- recorder,
- conflict mediator,
- skeptic, and
- quality controller.

Nonproductive group behavior includes:

- dominating the discussions,
- attending only parts of group meetings,
- losing papers,
- being chronically absent from class or meetings,
- being unreliable,
- being overly critical or being afraid to disagree, and
- being reluctant to contribute.

Some helpful behaviors in a group are:

- listening carefully to others,
- including everyone,
- disagreeing in an agreeable way,
- contributing ideas,
- being respectful and patient, and
- checking for understanding.

Different approaches to an assignment that may be considered are the following:

- The entire group works together on every problem.
- First the entire group discusses every problem to get an idea, then individuals work the problems, and finally the group reviews the results.
- Subsets of the group work subsets of the problems, and then the entire group reviews the results.
- Everyone tries every problem, and then the group members compare results.
- The group divides the assignment among the individuals, and then the group reviews the results.
- The group divides the assignment.

This list of approaches leads to a discussion on which strategies are effective in producing good group homework and projects to submit, and which strategies are effective in helping all group members to understand and learn mathematics. The list is useful when the instructor is monitoring the groups later. When a group is struggling with the group assignments, the instructor frequently can successfully motivate a change for improvement by asking these students their operational method and level of satisfaction with the results.

Duration of the Groups

Most authors of this text believe that permanent groups should be used throughout the semester or quarter, except perhaps in the initial few weeks. We believe that stable groups encourage responsibility since most students seek peer approval. Also, we have observed that a camaraderie develops within a well-functioning group that is kept together over an extended time period. The students within a group learn to respect each other's strengths and weaknesses as well as to draw on each other's strengths. We find that students within stable groups usually have more productive discussions and that each member's learning is enhanced. In addition, a stable group does not have to face the pragmatic issue of finding regular meeting times outside class each time that new groups are formed.

In a class where the instructor has decided to use permanent groups, students can have valuable experiences in temporary groups during the first week or two of the semester. On the first day, the groups can be formed by having students in nearby seats discuss their answers to questions. At each of the next few class meetings, students can be randomly assigned to different groups so that each student works with a large subset of the class. In this way, students meet many other students and acquire some sense of how they might work with particular students.

A few authors prefer to reorganize the groups during the semester in certain classes for various reasons. High attrition or absenteeism rates in a class make permanent groups unreliable; on the other hand, many instructors have observed that membership in a permanent group tends to improve attendance. A very small class may function as a single group outside class but be divided temporarily for in-class activities. Some instructors are concerned that permanent groups may encourage unhealthy competitiveness among the groups. Some think that the experience of working with different students is more valuable than the experience of working with one group over an extended period of time.

Over half of the respondents to the CLUME Survey reported that they usually maintain groups for a whole semester or quarter, and some maintain these groups for two semesters. Some respondents rearrange groups after half a semester or quarter, and others form groups for a single project. We can conclude that most of the authors and survey respondents usually form groups that remain stable over an extended period of time.

Size of the Groups

The size of the groups is a serious issue that must be resolved at the outset. While pairs of students work well for brief in-class activities, groups of three or four students usually are better for more challenging in-class activities, substantial homework assignments, and large projects.

The authors and respondents to the CLUME Survey have had experience with groups of two to five students. Many instructors vary the size of the groups that they use to accommodate the special circumstances in different classes. All but a few of the survey respondents reported that they used groups of different sizes, but four was most frequently checked as a size they used. Their reasons to avoid smaller groups included the extremely small size when one student withdraws from the course or is absent as well as the lack of diversity of ideas and strengths within a small group. The respondents' most frequently mentioned reasons to avoid larger groups were the difficulty of scheduling group meetings, the division of work, and the possibility of some members shirking work. The authors have observed groups of five that split into a trio and a pair who held separate discussions in class and who scheduled separate meetings outside class.

Formation of the Groups

The membership of the groups is a major decision that greatly affects the class throughout the lifetime of the groups. Each of the various methods for forming the groups has advantages, disadvantages, and advocates. The authors have tried the following methods of forming the cooperative learning groups.

1. Random Selection:

Students are assigned to groups by where they sit, by cards they draw from a prepared deck, by numbers as they "count off," by model of calculator, or by consecutive names on the class list. This quick method usually produces heterogeneous groups of students. It is a good way to form temporary groups, such as those used at the beginning of a course before permanent groups are formed. It eliminates the need for subjective judgments by the instructor. However, this method may produce groups skewed in ability, groups with personality conflicts, or groups with incompatible schedules.

2. Pseudo-Random Selection:

The instructor makes a few adjustments to randomly selected groups. Usually instructors should prepare the selection prior to class so those students do not see the adjustments being made.

3. Instructor Selection:

The instructor assigns groups based on information about the students. Often this information is collected by a questionnaire that requests the student's name, major and minor, residence, S.A.T. or A.C.T. scores, previous mathematics courses, calculator or computer experience, preferred group members, and possible meeting times. Some instructors use personality inventories, such as the Myers-Briggs Test; such tests require help from a counselor or other qualified professional.

When forming groups, the instructor should consider several factors. A heterogeneous group is more likely to have diverse ideas and approaches to a given problem. A group of very strong or very weak students often creates problems and challenges. A group with extreme differences of talent or academic background may also have problems.

If group work outside class is required, the most critical issue is the ease with which students in a group can arrange their meetings. Since commuting students may have greater time conflicts than resident students, the commuters usually should not be placed in the same group. On the other hand, commuting students who live near each other could be grouped together. Students living in the same dormitory find it easy to meet. About two-thirds of the CLUME Survey respondents reported that they do expect student groups to work outside class. Some mentioned that they have considered common meeting time, especially for commuters, when forming groups.

This method requires more work of the instructor than the other methods, but it may prevent difficulties such as time conflicts within a group or groups skewed in ability. However, students with incompatible personalities may inadvertently be placed in the same group.

4.   Student Selection:

After working with a variety of students and participating in a class discussion of group operations, the students select their own groups. The instructor should set some parameters for these selections, such as the range of acceptable sizes for the groups. Some instructors have suggested not allowing foreign students to congregate in a single group so that they do not become isolated from the rest of the class. However, if English fluency is a concern, students who speak a common language may be allowed to work in their own groups. As part of the selection process, students considering forming a group should ensure that there are times when their group is able to meet.

Students can make these decisions either inside or outside the classroom. If the selection takes place in class, students can write down one or two of their greatest strengths and weaknesses as well as a schedule of possible meeting times. Then the students circulate around the room to find a group of the required size.

Students tend to select others whom they know already. This avoids some initial awkwardness, and the group typically becomes productive quickly, particularly in an upper-level course with students who have known each other in several courses. Sometimes students select the group that they sat with on the first day of the course without considering more important criteria. A potential danger is a group composed entirely of weaker students, who may become discouraged. There may be a few students who are either too shy or too passive to find a group by the deadline. In this case, the instructor can help these students approach an established group. If there are enough of these unattached students, they may become a group by default, but often such groups have problems.

There was widespread support among the respondents to the CLUME Survey for each of the four specific methods of group formation listed. Over a third of the respondents reported that their students form their own groups, and almost as many respondents said that they assign students to groups. Almost one-fourth of the respondents use a combination of these two methods, and a few use some other methods. Among those who assigned groups, the most frequent criteria are common free time for group meetings, previous mathematics

courses, gender, and the results of some random process. The majority who assigned the groups formed heterogeneous groups with respect to the criteria, except, of course, times available for group meetings outside class.

The authors have learned that there is no group formation method that is effective in all situations. Instructors can promote group meetings outside class by making these meetings as convenient as possible for students, especially for commuting students, by forming groups of students who have common free time and who live near each other. Many factors, in addition to the way the groups are formed, affect the potential for success of any particular group of students in a mathematics class.

Maintaining and Monitoring Groups

After the cooperative learning groups have been formed in a class, and after the excitement of introductions and initial activities, the groups' functioning can be enhanced by further support and guidance through their lifetime. Ideally each group develops a sense of unity, a camaraderie that leads to mutual support and productive work. The instructor should encourage this development by setting clear expectations, by promoting the students' understanding of group dynamics, and by reinforcing desired behaviors. With specific instruction on behavior within a group and careful monitoring of the groups, instructors usually can forestall the development of insurmountable problems. However, although members of most groups work well together, some problems do occur. Instructors usually are able to guide the students in addressing their own problem within the group. On rare occasions, when attempts to resolve the problems fail, groups can be reorganized to avoid jeopardizing the learning of mathematics by their members.

Before addressing the issues here, we consider several group problems encountered by one of the authors. The first problem involved a group of five students in a sophomore Discrete Mathematics class. In hindsight, the groups probably should have been organized differently. During the first week of classes, the other students had made requests for specific groups, each with four students. When these requests were granted, there were just five students remaining, and these were assigned to one group. The relatively large size of the group, and the fact that these students did not know each other well made it somewhat difficult for this group to function on a high level immediately. The group members seemed to interact effectively in class, but their work on the first few outside weekly assignments was deficient. Some students wrote in their journals that the group was unable to find a common time to meet and that the submitted work was not a group effort. During a meeting with four of the group members and the instructor, the students again stated that they could find no meeting time. Actually they had discussed only a few different hours, and then they had given up. At the instructor's suggestion, one student wrote a week's calendar grid on the chalkboard, and then each of the four students crossed out the times that he could not meet. There were many hours left blank. Then one of the students offered to copy the grid and talk to the fifth student about his schedule. The group work improved significantly after this meeting. In this case, the instructor was able to offer a practical solution to finding a meeting time, and the students then were able to solve their problem themselves. Also, during the conversation, the general nature of group work and the value of participation were discussed.

In another situation, the instructor observed that members of a group of four Calculus I students were not interacting much during class or laboratory, and two of the members were absent several times during the first weeks of classes. In addition, the group's submitted projects were poor. One concerned student in the group sought individual help from the instructor, the department's free tutoring room, and students living near him in the dormitory. He wrote in his journal about his group's unresponsiveness, and finally he made a request to change to another group with several members who lived nearby in his dormitory. Actually, one very talented student in the new group had been explaining the work to him. Several students in the first group did not attend the group's meeting with the instructor, and generally they showed little interest in learning. Since the concerned student effectively already had joined the second group, the instructor agreed to the change. The three remaining students continued to do minimal work during the semester, and the student who changed his group was happier.

These two cases illustrate several typical group problems and possible resolutions. The reluctant or timid student, with encouragement and supervision, can become a productive group member who participates in his or her learning. The apathetic and unmotivated student sometimes will respond positively to a group setting. But that is by no means assured, and two or more such students may doom the group to failure. The issue of conflicts regarding meeting times is a critical one, but it is often more perceived than real, and it does provide a convenient excuse to the reluctant participant.

Desired behaviors can be reinforced by the instructor in class or laboratory by circulating through the room and privately or publicly praising the members of any group working well together. A group exam or a group component to an exam early in the semester can be a bonding event that encourages the students both to take responsibility for each others' learning in order to build a strong team and to learn the material well in order to contribute to the group's success. The same effect may be achieved by adding a few extra points to individual test scores for excellent or greatly improved performances of all members of a group. The instructor conveys a sense that group work is important by keeping the students aware of her monitoring of the groups' behavior and achievements.

As a way of preventing problems, instructors can encourage students to reflect on the productive group behavior discussed at the beginning of the course as it relates to their own experiences in their groups. The students' awareness is raised by questions to be answered in the early journal entries or in short reports written as part of each group assignment. Such questions can include:

- Did our group meet?
- Did everyone come on time?
- Did all participate?
- Did anyone dominate the discussion?
- Did our group answer at least one question in class?
- Did everyone in our group understand the group's solutions?
- Did group members ask each other for explanations?
- Were clear explanations given?
- In what ways did we work together well today?
- What should we do differently next time?

The questions above, except for the first one, can be used for group processing, which is the evaluation and discussion of the groups' functioning immediately after an episode of group work. Several minutes of group processing at the end of class can produce major improvements in group participation and cooperation. Group processing is especially effective at first, and it may be used only occasionally later in the semester after most groups seem to have absorbed the principles of good cooperative functioning.

Most respondents to the CLUME Survey give instruction in cooperative learning, either initially or throughout the duration of the class. They use a variety of methods to monitor the cooperative learning groups in their classes. Most use informal observation of the students' interactions within their groups during classes, laboratory sessions, and office visits. Less than half of these instructors use formal meetings with the groups, questionnaires, or student journals. Other techniques mentioned for monitoring groups included having students write short reports or fill in daily class participation forms. Some instructors communicate via email with their students about their groups. The essential idea here is that the groups should be observed and that the students should be aware that the instructor is concerned with the group process. The fact of the observation keeps students on task during laboratory sessions and classes; the instructor can stand near a group that seems to be having a prolonged social conversation.

Any instructor who uses cooperative learning in several classes is likely to encounter some of the standard forms of nonproductive behavior. Respondents to the CLUME Survey reported most frequently that they had observed students did not contribute to discussions, students who did not attend meetings, and groups that could not find a common meeting time. Less frequently encountered problems included: division of work by students without subsequent interaction, domination of discussions by one student, unwillingness of students to meet outside class, excessive absences of students, refusal to participate in group work, and, in rare cases, rejection of one student by all other members of the group. Notice that several different types of problems involve meetings outside scheduled classes and laboratory periods. In fact, some problems related to meetings outside class will not occur at all if available free time is one of the main criteria of group selection.

When we discuss problems within groups, we do not intend to indicate that every group, or even every class, has problems. An instructor can work to avoid problems that typically occur, and problematical situations that do develop usually can be improved.

Conclusions

In this chapter on practical implementation issues, we find that instructors make initial decisions that greatly affect cooperative learning in their classrooms. We recommend that instructors:

- find ways to use their classroom and laboratory configurations effectively for cooperative learning,
- engage students in introductory group activities and discussions on cooperative learning during the first class meetings,
- form groups for an extended period of time, such as for the semester after the first few weeks,
- assign three or four students to each group, and
- use students' schedules and residences as the main considerations for group membership in any class where students are expected to meet outside scheduled classroom and laboratory hours.

In addition, we recommend that instructors carefully monitor groups and discuss the process of cooperative learning with their students throughout the course in order to avoid problems within groups and to promote effective group interaction.

Chapter 3

Classroom Strategies for Cooperative Learning

**William E. Fenton, Barbara E. Reynolds, Neil A. Davidson,
Bernadette M. Baker, Ruth Berger, Anthony M. Szpilka**

What This Chapter Is About

In this chapter we present a variety of simple techniques for implementing cooperative activities in the classroom. Many have a straightforward structure, making them good beginning steps for those—students and faculty—whose experience with cooperative learning is limited. The techniques are flexible and amenable to myriad variations, qualities that make it possible to adapt them for use in a variety of physical settings, class sizes, pedagogical purposes, and time periods.

The class time needed for each technique varies from just a few minutes to an entire class period. But typically, each requires only a portion of the session. The remainder of the time might be devoted to additional cooperative activities, to faculty presentation of new material, to discussion of results by the entire class, or to a whole array of activities that engage the students in learning mathematics.

In addition to descriptions and examples of classroom strategies, this chapter presents suggestions for getting started with cooperative learning strategies, a brief guide to choosing an appropriate strategy for a specific topic, plus tips on designing or adapting problems for a group setting.

We presume that the student groups are already in place. The serious issues of how to form groups were considered in the previous chapter and will not be repeated here. Nor do we plan to discuss assessment in a group setting, except when it is particularly relevant to a specific cooperative learning technique. (Assessment issues will be discussed in the next chapter.) Our focus in this chapter is strictly on day-to-day classroom activities.

Getting Started with Cooperative Learning Strategies

Changing the way we teach—particularly for successful teachers with many years of experience—is hard work. Here are a few suggestions for getting started. And remember that change is a gradual process, not an event, so don't try to change everything all at once.

- Start with a class that you think will respond favorably to cooperative learning. When you feel comfortable in this one situation, consider expanding to additional courses. Some instructors may not want to switch immediately from lecture-based teaching to only group work, but would rather start slowly by using groups for cooperative review, short in-class discussions, or weekly group homework assignments.
- Select one simple cooperative learning strategy to use in your class. Use this strategy repeatedly until you and your students are comfortable with it. Then select a second cooperative learning strategy and begin to

implement that one repeatedly. The first strategy should continue to be used, but no longer as the sole method. Continue this process, adding one new strategy at a time.

• When implementing a cooperative learning strategy, give very clear, step-by-step directions and check to make sure that students understand. Worksheets or handouts may be beneficial. These directions are crucial for the first few times that students try a given strategy; once they are experienced with it, directions can be minimal. The instructor needs to be flexible and sensitive to the class. If a question baffles most students, the instructor should resist the temptation to answer it directly; instead restate and redirect the question to the groups, or ask a simpler version, or ask a question leading up to the original question.

• If an activity is not completed in the class period, the expectation that it be completed outside of class before the next class period, either individually or as a group, should be clear and explicit.

• Having each group choose a name for itself can promote a sense of unity and group identity. In addition, it gives the instructor an easy way to call on groups in class. A caveat is that the name should impart a positive image (so "Dazed and Confused" is not acceptable) and the name should be appropriate to say aloud in class.

• Look for opportunities within the regular curriculum to use groups. Some of the time normally spent in lecture or traditional testing can be changed into group work. Look for regular textbook problems that lend themselves to one of the strategies. Some texts are specifically designed to encourage cooperative learning, but even a traditional textbook will contain topics adaptable to group work.

• Expect that group activities will not necessarily go smoothly at first; it usually takes several weeks for students to begin functioning well in groups, even if the instructor is experienced and confident in using cooperative learning.

• An instructor new to cooperative learning may worry that group activities can allow weaker students to hide behind stronger ones and that an instructor might lose his sense of how well individual students understand the material. Our experience is that in most cases just the opposite

occurs. The increased involvement demanded by cooperative learning makes students' strengths and weaknesses more readily apparent. From watching the groups at work, an observant instructor usually will have a strong sense of who understands what, and how well. This is frequently apparent to other students as well, providing a strong motivation for greater efforts. Many of the strategies discussed below provide rich opportunities for observing what students know and what they can do, either individually or collectively. More informally, wandering around and listening to students' working conversations can be very illuminating. At first this may inhibit the dialog, but if done regularly, students soon will learn to ignore the instructor (a disquieting but probably healthy phenomenon).

• Consider informing your colleagues about what you are doing and why you are doing it. If possible find a supportive colleague who will try similar methods. Two faculty members working together can provide mutual support and can collaborate on designing activities. Even if your colleague isn't using cooperative learning in his own classes, having someone to talk to about your efforts to implement new pedagogical strategies is valuable.

After some time, many faculty members experience a qualitative leap in their comfort and ability with cooperative learning. They spontaneously begin to mix and match structures to fit their own personal style and the particular constraints of their teaching situation. This can create a dynamic and exciting classroom environment.

It is most helpful to have a small cadre of cooperative learning enthusiasts in your department or faculty. This team can provide enthusiasm, offer ideas for implementing cooperative learning, share experiences and classroom activities, organize seminars on cooperative structures, and observe and coach upon request. But don't be constrained by the nonexistence of such a group. Every department needs a few pioneers!

Classroom Strategies for Cooperative Learning

In this section we offer some cooperative learning strategies that we have found particularly successful in our own classes. We begin with some simple strategies, then present progressively more complex ones. This list of strategies is by no means complete. We have selected from among those strategies that have been successful for us, and we have attempted to give sufficient information to enable others to use these strategies successfully as well. There is a great deal of research and literature on specific cooperative learning techniques, and we encourage the reader to explore further.

Each strategy is accompanied by examples of how it can be employed for different courses in the undergraduate mathematics curriculum. Almost all of these examples were taken from the class notes of the authors and other cooperative learning practitioners, so the examples have been field-tested. Be aware that many of these examples can be used with several different strategies. For instance, the classroom examples for Think-Pair-Share will work well for Numbered-Heads Reporting, and vice versa, and they will work for other strategies as well.

As much as possible, the presentation of each strategy includes the following components:

- a short description of the technique, with possible variations of the basic strategy and some issues to consider;
- some typical uses of the strategy;
- an indication of the process skills it promotes or requires;
- sample questions applicable to the strategy.

Think-Pair-Share

Description

A question or problem is posed to the class. Students think individually and silently about a response for some period of time, then pair with another student to discuss the question and reach consensus. Pairs may then share their agreed-upon answers with another pair or with the rest of the class.

Students can be asked to work in groups rather than in pairs, then share with the entire class (Think-Group-Share). This is particularly fruitful for higher-level questions or questions with multiple responses.

In Bill Fenton's Mathematics for Elementary Education course (spring 1998), a student group created the following variation: The class was divided in half. The groups in each half worked one problem from a pair of similar problems. Then each group sent a representative to a group in the other half to share their work.

If the sharing takes place with the entire class, the instructor can prepare a quasi-randomized list of groups to call on. The random aspect reduces complacency, since any group can be chosen at any time, but the list can be structured to allow every group an equal number of opportunities over time.

If a response from a group is incorrect or incomplete, try to redirect the question back to the groups in a nonjudgmental way.

The instructor must decide whether the sharing is to be done in pairs, in trios, or in quartets. This might vary from problem to problem, depending on the nature of the questions. Classroom factors such as table size or whether there is room to arrange desks in clusters may also influence this decision.

Typical Uses

- Discuss concepts, general ideas, or procedures.
- Brainstorm.
- Clarify issues.
- Solve problems.
- Identify confusion or misunderstandings.
- Provide a foundation for later class discussion.
- Encourage discussion in a large class setting.

Process Skills

Students asked to use the Think-Pair-Share strategy learn to organize their thoughts before speaking. They improve at asking meaningful questions within the pair or group. They practice interpreting written material from the text, the instructor, or other students. The students see that there can be multiple ways to solve a problem, and they create alternative approaches to a problem. Further, the pair or group learns to reach consensus on their work.

Examples for Think-Pair-Share

- Developmental Mathematics or Basic Algebra

  – Defining Terms: What is meant by the term reciprocal? Include an example in your explanation.

  – Solving Equations: For the equation $\frac{5}{x-3} = \frac{2}{x+3}$, what values cannot be solutions? How can you tell without actually solving the equation?

- Mathematics for Elementary Education

  – Defining Addition: (The class is shown a picture with three solid triangles, one solid square, and four hollow squares.) This diagram shows four solid objects and five squares. Hence "$4 + 5 = 8$." Explain why this doesn't work, using set language and a Venn diagram in your explanation.

  – Perimeter and Area: Draw at least four rectangles that have a perimeter of 12. Calculate the area of each rectangle. Follow-up: Repeat with "perimeter" and "area" reversed.

- Elementary Statistics

  – Scatterplots: Here are some data (for instance, average temperature versus total precipitation for the months in a given year). Use your graphing calculator to create a scatterplot of these data. Is there a relationship between the two variables?

  – Probability Distributions: What is the average number of days in a month?

- Discrete Mathematics

  – Propositional Calculus: n mod 15 is odd, and n is relatively prime to 15 or n div 15 is even. With $n = 35$ is this true or false, and why? Follow-up question: Find a value for n that makes the sentence true.

  – Permutations: How many permutations can be made of the set $\{1, 2, 3, 4\}$? How many 4-permutations can be made from the set $\{1, 2, ..., 10\}$? In general, how many k-permutations can be made from a set having n elements? (This is a sequence of tasks.)

- Precalculus

  – Factor Theorem: Give an example of a quadratic or higher degree equation with 5 as a solution and then solve the equation completely.

  – Intersecting Curves: How many points of intersection can occur between the graph of a quadratic polynomial and a circle? Illustrate your answer with drawings and equations.

- Calculus

  – Critical Numbers: If $f'(c) = 0$, what can you say about the behavior of the function at $(c, f(c))$?

  – Interpreting Integrals: The function $g(t)$ gives the rate at which folks arrive at McDonalds for time from 0 to 24 hours. What is a practical interpretation of the integral $\int_{11}^{14} g(t)\, dt$?

- Linear Algebra

  – Coordinates: The vectors $Q_1 = [3, 4]'$ and $Q_2 = [-1, 2]'$ form a basis for $\mathbf{R}^2$. Draw the axes and label the quadrants for the Q-coordinate system.

  – Row Operations: On the board is an augmented matrix (perhaps a 3×4 matrix in the form $[A\,|\,B]$ with A of rank 2). Page xx of the text describes the three elementary row operations. The goal is to use these row operations to reduce the matrix to a simpler form.

    Note: This is a sequence of questions, each requiring a response from the groups. Here is the first step of the reduction. What operations were used to get this? Here is the second step. What operations were used? *Etc.*, until reduced echelon form is reached. What are the equations for this reduced matrix? What is the solution to the system?

- Advanced Topics

  – Differential Equations: A raindrop collects moisture at a rate that is proportional to its surface area. Express this situation with a differential equation.

– Group Theory: Let G be a commutative group and let a and b be elements of G that have orders 2 and 3, respectively. Does G necessarily have an element of order 6? Give a proof or counterexample.

– Topology: Prove that if a function on a compact topological space is continuous, then it is uniformly continuous.

Think-Share-Write

Description

This is an expanded variation of Think-Pair-Share with an emphasis on individual assessment. Students are given one or several questions. They think about these questions individually for a few minutes, to formulate solution strategies. They then share their ideas collectively for another defined period of time. After that each student writes up individual answers.

During the individual thinking time, it is important to keep student writing to a minimum. Otherwise some students may begin their write-up of the question individually. During the discussion phase, everyone should be encouraged to speak in their group—to ask a question, to give ideas, or to comment on someone else's idea. Again, it is important that the actual write-up of the answers does not occur here. Some faculty insist that no writing take place during the "think" or "share" steps.

Think-Share-Write can be combined with Group Critique (see below) by passing the completed papers to other groups for comments and corrections. In this case, papers can be identified solely by group name, or not identified at all. Another variation is for each group to review the individual papers written by its members, then select the best one to pass along or to submit to the instructor.

The papers could be collected and graded, as an alternative approach to a quiz. The potential advantages of this method include getting better quality responses than a standard quiz, plus having learning take place during the quiz. However, this approach will take more time than the usual quiz format. Grades on these papers can be assigned by

individual scores, by a score based on the average of individual scores within the group, or by other methods.

Typical Uses

• Check for understanding of a critical concept.

• At the beginning of class, check on homework completion.

• At the end of class, check for understanding of that day's work.

• Generate multiple approaches for solving a particular problem.

• Take a quiz or exam that draws on both group and individual knowledge.

Process Skills

While using Think-Share-Write, students learn to share their ideas and to compare alternative methods for solving a problem. They gain experience at interpreting the meaning of an answer or a calculation. During the individual writing phase, students learn to organize their thoughts before writing and to create clear responses. They also improve their ability to use mathematical notation correctly.

Examples for Think-Share-Write

• Developmental Mathematics or Basic Algebra

– Common Multiples: Explain how you can find the least common multiple for a pair of numbers. What is the least common multiple of 36, 84, and 90?

– Factoring an Expression: Factor the expression $x^2 + ax + bx + ab$. Explain in words the method you used to do this factoring.

• Mathematics for Elementary Education

– Area: Explain why the formula $A = b \cdot h$ works for parallelograms. Include a properly labeled diagram.

– Number Properties: Addition of whole numbers has some important properties: associative, closure, commutative, identity.

Which of these properties does subtraction of whole numbers have? Justify your answers.

- Elementary Statistics

  – Design of Experiments: Is addition faster by paper and pencil or by calculator? Design an experiment your group can do to answer this question. Note: The class can agree on one design, then perform the experiment in class. One instructor arranged this experiment so that the problems in the first trial used no carrying, while those in the second trial used a great deal of carrying. This caused strikingly different results and led to a discussion of bias.

  – Central Limit Theorem: Explain how the Central Limit Theorem is used when calculating a confidence interval from a large sample.

- Discrete Mathematics

  – Quantification: The Well-Ordering Principle for **R** says that if a set of real numbers is finite, then the set must have a smallest element. What quantifiers can you find in this statement? Write this statement in mathematical notation.

  – Mathematical Induction: When constructing a mathematical induction proof, it is necessary to find a base case for which the proposition is true. Explain what this means and why it is necessary, including examples.

- Precalculus

  – Graphing: Write a complete description explaining how to graph a function.

  – Periodicity: Find all x-intercepts of $y = 5\cos(3x + \frac{\pi}{4})$.

- Calculus

  – Interpreting the Derivative: Consider the statement: "Newton's method is an application of local linearity." Explain in precise terms why you agree or disagree.

  – Integration Notation: Suppose that F is an antiderivative function for f, and $F(a)$ and $F(b)$ are real numbers. The claim is made that $\int_a^b f(x)\, dx = F(a) - F(b)$.

Do you agree? Explain fully, including appropriate examples or sketches.

- Linear Algebra

  – Subspaces: Every subspace of $\mathbf{R}^3$ will contain the origin. Write a proof of this statement.

  – Rank and Nullity: Theorem: For any matrix A, $\text{rank}(A) + \dim(\text{nullspace}(A))$ equals the number of columns of A. Explain why this is true.

- Advanced Topics

  – Group Theory: Let $(G, *)$ be a group, $t \in G$, and t' its inverse. Consider the binary operation $*'$ defined on G by $a *' b = a * b * t'$. Prove or disprove: $(G, *')$ is again a group.

  – Topology: State two definitions of compactness and prove that they are equivalent.

Numbered-Heads Reporting

Description

Each student in the group is assigned a number, from 1 to the number of people in the group. A question, issue, or problem is posed and students discuss it within the group. An individual from a group is called on by number to report on the thinking of the group.

The students should be told in advance that one number will be announced but not which one. The number is announced after the discussions and it can be randomly selected. Rolling a die is a dramatic way to do so. The randomness encourages everyone to be prepared to respond.

If the question has multiple answers or several components to the answer, the individual with the selected number can respond from every group. They either can answer in turn or can come to the board to write their group's response(s). Another method is for the first student responding to choose a group and/or number for the next response, and so on.

Other group members may wish to elaborate on the speaker's comments after she is finished. The instructor should decide in advance whether to allow this, for it can affect the dynamic and quality of the group's discussion.

Typical Uses

- Discuss concepts or solve problems in a way that holds the group responsible for each member's understanding.
- Identify confusion or misunderstanding.
- Check for understanding of individuals within the group.

Process Skills

Numbered-Heads Reporting promotes many of the process skills of Think-Group-Share and Think-Share-Write. But students who know that they can be asked to speak for the group may be more attentive and more questioning under this strategy. They may ask for more complete and clearer explanations from others in the group. The added emphasis on individual accountability encourages active participation from everyone.

Examples for Numbered-Heads Reporting

- Developmental Mathematics or Basic Algebra
    - Division by Zero: Explain why it is not possible to divide by zero.
    - Quadratic Equations: Write an equation for a parabola that opens upwards and graph it. Explain how you could change this equation so that the graph would be a parabola opening downwards.
- Mathematics for Elementary Education
    - Symmetry: Draw a quadrilateral that is not a square. Then find all of its symmetries. The representatives can come to the board simultaneously to record their answers.
    - Polygons: Draw a Venn diagram showing the relationships between the sets of squares, rectangles, rhombuses, parallelograms, trapezoids, and kites. What universe are you using?

- Elementary Statistics
    - Sampling Distributions: Consider a normally distributed population with a standard deviation of 10. Find the standard deviation of the sampling distributions for samples of sizes 10, 20, 30, 40, and 50. What happens, and what does this mean for the distributions?
    - Binomial Distributions: According to the 1990 U. S. Census, 34% of Kentucky adults did not finish high school. In a random sample of forty Kentucky adults, what is the probability that less than half of them finished high school?
- Discrete Mathematics
    - Pigeonhole Principle: If you pick natural numbers at random, how many must you pick to guarantee that two of them are equivalent mod 10? Justify your answer.
    - Mathematical Induction: Here is a recursive function: $a(1) = 1$; $a(k) = (13 \cdot a(k-1)) \bmod 50$. Find $a(1), a(2), \ldots, a(5)$. Will $a(k)$ always be an odd number? Prove your answer.
- Precalculus
    - Simultaneous Nonlinear Equations: Give equations of a pair of quadratic equations that do not intersect each other. How do you know that they never intersect?
    - Graphing: Sketch the graphs of various functions that have the following behavior on the interval $[0, 10]$:

        increasing on $[0, 10]$;

        decreasing on $[0, 10]$;

        increases on $[0, 10]$ at a decreasing rate;

        increases on $[0, 10]$ at an increasing rate.

    Possible extension to these activities: Make up "stories" related to each of your functions.
- Calculus
    - Differentiation: Give examples of functions that are not differentiable at $x = 2$. Explain what is happening there in each example.

- Geometric Series: (These four problems are to be given in sequence.)

  – Factor each of the polynomials $x^2 - 1$, $x^3 - 1$, $x^4 - 1$, and $x^5 - 1$ into exactly two factors, one of which is linear.

  – Now factor the polynomial $x^n - 1$ into exactly two factors, one of which is linear.

  – Use your result to find the sum of a geometric progression $1 + x + x^2 + \cdots + x^n$.

  – (This requires the limit concept.) Investigate values of x for which the infinite geometric series $1 + x + x^2 + \cdots + x^n + \cdots$ converges and find a formula for its sum. For which values of x will it diverge? Why?

- Linear Algebra

  – Dimension: Here are three vectors in $\mathbf{R}^3$: $[1, 0, 4]^t, [-1, 4, 16]^t, [2, -1, 3]^t$. The span of these vectors is a subspace of $\mathbf{R}^3$. What is its dimension?

  – Linear Transformations: Recall that the line containing the points X and Y can be written $t \cdot X + (1-t) \cdot Y$. Simplify the expression $A(t \cdot X + (1-t) \cdot Y)$ and describe the result geometrically.

- Advanced Topics

  – Abstract Algebra: Commutativity can be interpreted as saying that in applying a binary operation to two elements, it does not matter in which order you take the elements. Give an analogous interpretation for associativity.

  – Abstract Algebra: First determine whether S_2 and S_3 are groups of permutations under the operation of composition. Make tables for each situation. Then prove or disprove that S_n, the set of all permutations of the set $\{1, 2, \ldots, n\}$, is a group under the operation of composition of functions. (This requires some lemmas about the composition of injective (one-to-one) functions, and so on.)

  – Topology: Prove the following statement: Any subset of the real line having the form $[a, b]$ is both connected and compact. Must every connected compact subset of the real line have this same form? Prove or disprove.

  – Topology: Give an example of a topological space that is homeomorphic to the real numbers with the usual topology and an example of one which is not. Explain your answers.

Data Sharing

Description

Each group performs a simple experiment to generate data for mathematical modeling. Groups then model their data and report their results to the rest of the class so that the results of all the models can be compared. Alternatively, the data may be pooled to form a single data set for every group to use.

Students often show a surprising interest in data they collect themselves. They may be astonished that data they collect can fit a predetermined model. They have a tendency to believe that these are data that the instructor and the textbook author couldn't anticipate—because, after all, the data belongs to the students themselves, not to the instructor or the textbook's author!

There is the possibility of surprises in the data, either because they were improperly collected or because some students find true outliers. For example, one instructor asked students for the number of doors in their house. The minimum reply was 4 and the maximum was 48. When queried, the student with the maximum replied that this figure included all closet and cupboard doors, which most students did not include. Once the question was made more specific the distribution was more reasonable, though 4 remained an outlier.

Typical Uses

- Generate a large amount of data quickly.

- Explore a variety of examples of the same mathematical concept.

- Determine which parameters are important and which are irrelevant for a particular mathematical model.

Classroom Strategies

Process Skills

Data Sharing requires a student group to recognize a common goal and to work toward it. Usually the students must assume various roles, such as recorder or timekeeper, and they must coordinate their work.

Examples for Data Sharing

- Elementary Statistics

    – Confidence Intervals: I want to estimate the mean time it takes to print one's name. Collect some data in your group and calculate a *t*-interval with 90% confidence. Follow-up discussion: Write all of these intervals on the board and notice the varying answers. Pool the data and do a class-wide estimate; compare to the earlier results.

    – Hypothesis Testing: I think the typical person takes at least three seconds longer to print her name with the non-dominant hand. What are the hypotheses? Collect some data and do a *t*-test. Find the *p* value and draw a conclusion.

- College Algebra or Precalculus

    – Mathematical Modeling: Give each group of students a spring, which they can mount vertically next to a meter stick and a set of weights. Have them collect data on the position of the bottom of the spring *vs.* the amount of weight they have hung on it. Then ask them to plot these data and find the equation of a line that fits them as well as possible. When groups present their results to the class, one can generate an interesting discussion about the significance of the slope and the *y*-intercept, especially if different groups were given springs of the same stiffness (spring constant) which would therefore yield the same slope.

- Linear Algebra

    – Independence: (For a class with $n+1$ groups.) Each group makes up a vector from $\mathbf{R}^n$ and writes it on the board. These vectors could be based on birthdates, digits from Social Security numbers, *etc.,* or could be selected arbitrarily. Then the groups decide if the resulting collection of vectors

is independent. (If vectors are selected arbitrarily, groups may make simplistic choices such as $[1, 0, \ldots, 0]$. Perhaps a restriction should be stated, such as not allowing any two entries to be equal.)

Board Work

Description

The groups go to the board to solve a problem, with one person chosen as the scribe for the group. The scribe is responsible not for solving the problem, merely for recording the group's work. After the groups have finished their work at the board, the class should review the results. This can be brief or extensive, depending on the particular problems and the groups' results.

All groups could do the same problem, or each group could have its own problem. In the latter situation, time could be allowed for each group to present its work. The set of problems can be interrelated in some way, in which case the class can discuss the results and seek the connection.

It may happen that a group is unable to complete its problem or is taking an excessive amount of time. The instructor could help this group or could ask another group, or the entire class, to help. This should be done in a constructive way, to avoid embarrassing the struggling group.

Typical Uses

- Compare multiple approaches to a problem.
- Compare related problems.
- Solve multi-step problems.
- Construct proofs.

Process Skills

A group working at the board must give clear explanations of ideas and must listen carefully to each other. The group must reach consensus quickly on a strategy for solving the problem and then agree on the correctness of their solution. Standing together seems to add urgency to their work.

Examples for Board Work

- Mathematics for Elementary Education

  – Other Bases: Here is a set of arithmetic problems in base 5. Work your designated problem.

  – Divisibility: Give a definition of "even number." The scribe for each group writes their definition on the board, and the class is asked to consider whether these definitions are equivalent. The instructor may then ask each group to demonstrate or prove that their definition is equivalent to one other definition. Follow-up question: Give a definition of "odd number."

- Elementary Statistics

  – Graphing Data: Here is a set of data. (Each group is given one copy of the data set, perhaps generated by the class.) Decide in your group how to graph this data set and draw your graph on the board. Be prepared to explain why you chose this type of graph.

  – Binomial Distributions: For a class having n groups, have each group calculate the probability of 0, 1, …, or n successes in n trials with a given probability p of success on each trial. (The value of n should be large enough that every group will have one or more calculations to perform.) Some groups could do two or more of the easier calculations, or each group could do both an easy and a more difficult calculation. If the experiment has $p = \frac{1}{2}$, like tossing coins, a group could be assigned the computations for k and $n - k$.

- Discrete Mathematics

  – Venn Diagrams: Draw a Venn diagram for $S \cup T = S$, for $S \cap T = S$, for $S - T = S$, for $T - S = S$.

  – Pascal's Identity: Using a specified n-value, each group computes

  $$\binom{n}{k}, \binom{n-1}{k}, \binom{n-1}{k-1}$$

  for an assigned value or values of k. For instance, using $n = 11$ each group would calculate these quantities for one or two

values from $k = 1, …, 10$. Once all the data are posted, the instructor can point out the relationship between these quantities and then state the theorem. (Alternatively, the instructor can invite the students to discuss the data in their groups, and to formulate conjectures about the relationships they observe.)

- Precalculus

  – Properties of Polynomial Functions: Using such mathematical terminology as domain, range, roots, turning points, intercepts, and asymptotic behavior, (a) list on one part of the board properties that all cubic polynomials must exhibit, and (b) list on another part of the board properties that they might exhibit. Then generate examples of cubics that do and do not exhibit the properties listed in (b).

  – Graphing Cyclic Functions: Here is an equation for a cyclic function. (Each group is given its own sine or cosine function.) On the board draw a graph of your group's function. (An interesting possibility is to include two seemingly different functions that have the same graph.)

- Calculus

  – Definite Integrals: Sketch a region which is bounded by two cubic functions and whose area is given by the integral

  $$\int_0^3 (9 - x^2)\, dx.$$

  – Integration: Several triple integrals are written on the board in which the integrands are the same expression but the orders of integration are different. Each group is asked to evaluate one of the integrals and put their answer on the board. Follow-up discussion: Does the order of integration make a difference? Is this always true?

- Linear Algebra

  – Determinants: For a given 3×3 matrix, each group does the cofactor expansion on a different row or column. The class compares the results and decides which computation was easiest.

  – Eigenvalues: Each group creates a 2×2 matrix. Perhaps the groups exchange their papers. Find the eigenvalues of your matrix. (Suggestion: Give some parameters for creating this matrix, to avoid getting the identity or other simplistic answers.)

- Advanced Topics

    – Abstract Algebra or Geometry: Each group is given an object such as a polygon or polyhedron and asked to write its symmetries and determine its symmetry group.

    – Combinatorics: The groups are asked to write a generating function for the number of ways to select r objects from a pile having three red balls, four green balls, and four white balls. Once agreement is reached, each group is asked to calculate on the board the appropriate coefficient for a different value of r.

    – Linear Programming: Each group is given a linear program using two decision variables and asked to draw the feasible region, to write the augmented form of the linear program, and to label the graph with the indicating variables. The problems could include degenerate or infeasible situations.

Roundtable (or Round Robin)

Description

Pose a question having multiple answers, or give each group a worksheet; in either case, a group uses only one piece of paper or worksheet. A student writes down one response, says it aloud, and then passes the paper or worksheet to the next person. The process continues in this way until the group runs out of ideas or until the instructor calls a break. A student may choose to pass on any round but should still be given the opportunity to respond the next time around.

One might also give a group of k students a set of k problems to solve simultaneously: students take turns adding one step at a time to the solution of each problem, after checking what was done at the previous step, as they keep passing the papers around the circle. For more difficult questions, the sheet of paper could be passed between groups rather than

between individuals within a group, with each group expected to add to the work.

When this strategy is used for brainstorming, students should be instructed not to comment on the responses being generated, as that tends both to slow the process and to stifle creativity. Instead, evaluation of the responses should take place only after the group has finished generating its list. If Roundtable is being used to review a topic, however, it might be appropriate to have each student evaluate the previous response before adding a new one.

After each group has completed its paper, it could be passed to another group for review or additions. (See Group Critique below.) Another option is for each group to send a representative to the board to write their responses, followed by a discussion by the entire class.

As an assessment tool, the group paper can be collected and perhaps evaluated for a grade. For individual accountability, the group can be asked to fold the paper in quarters with each student identifying her/his own quadrant; as the paper is passed around, students enter their examples in their own quadrant.

Group members often want to discuss each other's contributions as the Roundtable progresses. Depending on the task, it may be better to delay this until the end. However, a task in which one step relies on the previous step needs this immediate feedback. If mistakes occur, they could be corrected by others in the group, by other groups, or by the instructor.

While most students will be willing to participate, there is the possibility of an individual who consistently passes. If this continues for a significant length of time, the other group members may become frustrated and resentful. Building in some sort of individual accountability can act against this.

Typical Uses

- Brainstorm for new ideas.
- Generate examples.
- Apply or practice an idea or concept.
- Review concepts, terminology, or kinds of problem-solving strategies.

Process Skills

During Roundtable, each member of a group should be encouraged to present ideas without criticism. The others in the group must be able to listen carefully without interrupting the speaker. The group members must be able to take turns in an orderly way.

Examples for Roundtable (or Round Robin)

- General

    – Group Dynamics (in a discussion before groups are selected): What are desirable traits and behaviors for the members of your future group? How could a group approach an assignment? What are the advantages and disadvantages to each of these approaches? What are some potential difficulties to avoid?

    – Problem Solving: In your group, name three possible strategies for problem solving. Each group can report to the class.

- Developmental Mathematics or Basic Algebra

    – Equivalent Fractions: Given a particular fraction, write as many equivalent fractions as possible in a given time period.

    – Linear Equations: Sketch graphs of lines whose slopes are $\frac{2}{3}$, and give the equation of each.

- Mathematics for Elementary Education

    – Explaining Addition: As a group, draw a picture to explain $4 + 6$. Put your group's name on the paper and pass it to another group. On the paper you receive draw a picture for this problem that is different from the one shown. Repeat; eventually return the paper to its original group.

    – Hierarchy of Operations: You are allowed to insert parentheses into the arithmetic problem $3 \cdot 4 - 8 \div 2$. How many different values can your group find?

- Elementary Statistics

    – Probability: Suppose I have two dimes and three pennies in my pocket. If I pick one coin at random, then a second, and then a third, what are the possible outcomes?

    – Random Variables: (Each group is given a bag of M&Ms, as a source of data for that day's work.) What are some variables related to M&Ms? What type is each variable?

- Discrete Mathematics

    – *GCD* and *LCM*: Find pairs of natural numbers a and b so that $\gcd(a, b) = 30$ and $\operatorname{lcm}(a, b) = 2100$. Once you think you have found them all, explain why you think so.

    – Set Theory: Suppose $S = \{2, 4, 6, 8\}$. In your group list all the subsets of S that contain 8. Then list all the subsets that do not contain 8. Give a reason why there are the same number of each.

- Precalculus

    – Zeros: Write expressions for functions where 3 is a zero of the function.

    – Inverse of a Function: Describe different ways in which a function and its inverse function are related to each other.

- Calculus

    – Differentiation: Write down examples of functions whose derivatives must be computed using the chain rule.

    – Notation: Let f be a differentiable function with $y = f(x)$. In how many ways can you write an expression for the derivative of f with respect to x? Follow-up question: How can you indicate the derivative of f evaluated at $x = 3$?

- Linear Algebra

    – Linear Systems: Given a system of linear equations, the first person writes the augmented matrix. The second person checks this, then does one step of the Gauss-Jordan reduction. Continue. When everyone agrees that they are finished, the group writes the solution to the system.

    – Linear Transformations: Each group creates a 2×2 matrix A containing four different entries. Perhaps the groups exchange papers. The instructor draws the unit square on the board (in the first quadrant, in the natural way), but unlabeled.

Each person in turn selects a vertex V of this square, calculates AV, and plots the result. The group completes the drawing of the image, then copies A and their picture on the board.

- Advanced Topics

  – Abstract Algebra: Each group member in turn gives an example of a subgroup of S_4. Once the group feels that the list is complete, each person chooses a subgroup and decides if it is normal, or cyclic, or contains only even permutations, *etc.* Continue until all subgroups have been examined.

  – Topology: Give an example of a topological space that has (does not have) a property that the space of real numbers with the usual topology has (does not have). Note: This gives a total of four combinations.

Flock Around

Description

In this variant of Roundtable, several stations are set up around the classroom, using the chalkboard or large pieces of paper. At each station some mathematical concept is stated or a problem is posed that requires multiple steps for a complete solution. The goal is to list a property of the concept, to give an example of the concept, or to provide a step in the solution of the problem. Groups circulate around the classroom, given either a time limit (say, one minute between changes) or a certain amount of work each group must do on each sheet.

Giving each group a different color of chalk or pen allows an assessment to be made of each group's understanding of a particular concept.

Groups will work at differing rates. If the tasks are fairly short this will not be an issue, but longer tasks may result in some groups being idle while others continue to work. There is also the possibility of a group that is unable to complete its task.

Typical Uses

- Review concepts or definitions.
- Generate examples.
- Practice or master a skill or procedure.

Process Skills

The process skills for Flock Around are similar to those of Roundtable. The fact that the group's work is on public display may promote more careful review of its work.

Examples for Flock Around

- Developmental Mathematics or Basic Algebra

  – Polynomial Equations: Give an example of an equation that has 5 as a root and sketch the graph of your equation. What other roots does your equation have?

  – Linear Equations: Give an example of a linear equation whose slope is $\frac{2}{3}$. What is the root of your equation?

- Mathematics for Elementary Education

  – Common Divisors: List a common divisor of 84 and 350; of 660 and 3850; of 630 and 2100; *etc.* If there are no additional divisors at a particular station, explain why not.

  – Symmetry: For a given geometric object (triangle, parallelogram, cube, tetrahedron, cylinder, *etc.*), identify its various symmetries.

- Elementary Statistics

  – Probability: Given a small collection of objects (say, five or six items), list the different ways there are to choose (or choose and arrange) three of them.

  – Variable Types: The stations are labeled as Categorical, Quantitative and Discrete, Quantitative and Continuous, Bivariate, *etc.* As the groups circulate they add examples of the appropriate type of data.

- Discrete Mathematics

  – Implication: Each group is given a different statement involving an implication.

At each of three stations they are to write their statement and its: converse, contrapositive, or negation.

  – Set Theory: A set S is specified. At each station a group is to list a subset of S which has a stated property; they should then check that all the subsets given (their own and those of the previous groups) are different subsets. Eventually, a group may have to explain why all such subsets have been found. For instance, suppose S is $\{1, 2, \ldots, 10\}$. The properties at the stations could be: contains only primes, contains only multiples of 6, contains a divisor of 35, has exactly five elements, *etc.*

- Precalculus

  – Parallelism: Write an equation of a line parallel to a given line, and check that the example you are giving is different from those given by previous groups.

  – Asymptotes: Sketch graphs of functions with a horizontal asymptote of $y = 3$, a vertical asymptote at $x = 3$, a diagonal asymptote at $y = 2x$, *etc.* Try to find examples for which the function approaches the asymptote in a different way than the previous examples did.

- Calculus

  – Differentiation: Write down examples of functions whose derivatives must be computed using the chain rule, the quotient rule, or the product rule.

  – Limits: Sketch a portion of the graph for a function f where: the limit of f as $x \to 1$ from the left is 2; the limit of f as $x \to 0$ from the right is 2; the limit of f as $x \to \infty$ is 2; *etc.* Try to find as many variations on continuity and differentiability as possible.

- Advanced Topics

  – Abstract Algebra: At each station, the definition of an algebraic property is given. Each group is to come up with one example and one non-example.

  – Topology: Give an example of a topological space that has (does not have) a property that the space of real numbers with the usual topology has (does not have). Note: This gives a total of four combinations.

Short Writes (or One-Minute Papers)

Description

Short Writes are short written responses to specific questions. This is not exclusively a cooperative strategy; indeed, this strategy is used in many courses for quick assessment of student understanding and opinions. The "one" in one-minute is not to be taken too literally, although the brevity suggested by that reference is useful.

When used as a cooperative strategy, responses may be written individually after pairs or groups have consulted (reminiscent of Think-Share-Write) or they may be cooperatively authored. For accountability purposes, responses occasionally may be written and submitted individually, without prior discussion.

These papers can be written before presenting a topic to assess background knowledge or may be done after the topic has been studied at some length. It is sometimes useful to do a sample in both places. If the papers are used strictly to identify difficulties, they need not be graded. However, it may be necessary to include these papers in the overall grading scheme if the students are to take them seriously.

For assessment of the progress of individual students or groups, these responses can be accumulated over the course of the term. Over time, a general picture of the depth of understanding and typical difficulties often emerges. In addition, the sequence of papers shows the development of the student's ability to articulate conceptual material.

Students will need guidance in giving insightful responses. The quality of the responses to a question like "What is the main idea of this section?" may be improved by reading aloud or posting a few particularly good submissions. Some students need help distinguishing between an informative answer *vs.* a non-answer; *e.g.*, "It is about the derivative." Insisting on sentences rather than lists of words or of topics will help but is not sufficient. For example, the student who persists in giving responses like "It is about the derivative" could be asked to describe how the derivative is used in this situation, to tell why the derivative is relevant, *etc.*

The student who turns in a blank sheet is particularly worrying. That student could be asked to resubmit the paper—perhaps at greater length, since he will have extra time to work on it—or it may be appropriate to request that the student meet with the instructor outside of class.

Typical Uses

- At the beginning of class, check whether homework problems or readings have been understood.

- At the end of class, check that the important points of the session have been recognized.

- Obtain a quick snapshot that monitors current beliefs or understandings.

- Check where students are having difficulty with an idea or concept.

Process Skills

Short Writes require a student to reflect on her/his understanding and to write about it. This gives practice at explaining ideas and at using mathematical notation correctly. It may require the student to relate a concept to previous work. When a group discusses a question or concept before writing, the knowledge that each individual will have to present her/his thoughts can encourage careful listening and questioning.

Examples for Short Writes

- General

  - In a sentence or two, explain the main idea of this section (or lecture or example).

  - How can a particular mathematical object or fact be used?

  - What idea or concept is giving you the most trouble at this point? (Or, What are you confused about right now?)

  - In a sentence or two give the meaning of (some mathematical term).

  - What did you learn during this class?

(Or, What did you learn in reading this section?)

- Developmental Mathematics or Basic Algebra

  - Fractions: What is meant by "least common multiple"? Explain how the *LCM* is useful when adding or subtracting fractions.

  - Rational Expressions: When will a rational expression be undefined?

- Mathematics for Elementary Education

  - Similarity: What does "similar" mean for triangles? What does it mean for quadrilaterals?

  - Number Properties: Addition of whole numbers has some important properties: associative, closure, commutative, identity. Explain what each of these means.

- Elementary Statistics

  - Correlation: What would an r value near -1 mean?

  - Sampling: What are some advantages and disadvantages to using a sample instead of a census?

- Discrete Mathematics

  - Permutations and Combinations: Are there more combinations or permutations? Why?

  - De Morgan's Laws: Write an expression equivalent to $(A \cup B)^c$ and explain why the two expressions are equal.

- Precalculus

  - Odd and Even Functions: In a sentence or two, explain the meaning of the term "odd function."

  - Function Graphs: How can you use the graph of a function to solve an equation?

- Calculus

  - Functions and Their Derivatives: If you know the derivative of a function, can you find the function? Explain why or why not. Support your answer with examples.

  - Differentiability: How can you tell where a function is differentiable? In your answer, talk about functions represented as graphs and functions represented as expressions.

- Linear Algebra

    – Linear Equations: Write a sentence explaining what a linear equation is. Possible follow-up: Compare your group's answers and discuss. Read the explanation on page *xx* of the text.

    – Linear Dependence: Suppose $\{V_1, V_2, V_3\}$ is a set of vectors. What does it mean to say that this set is linearly dependent? Include an equation in your answer.

- Advanced Topics

    – Geometry: List at least three ways in which hyperbolic geometry differs from Euclidean geometry.

    – Abstract Algebra: If G is a cyclic group of order n and d is a divisor of n, does G have a subgroup of order d? Explain why or why not.

    – Linear Programming: The Fundamental Insight states that the columns under the slack variables keep a record of the pivoting in the Simplex Algorithm. Explain how this can be used to update a completed problem without re-solving it. Include the appropriate formulas.

    – Trees and Searching: Explain the difference between depth-first search and breadth-first search.

Groups/Pairs Exchange

Description

Each group or pair of students is asked to generate an example of some mathematical object. The example is then passed along to a second group or pair who responds in some way to the item received. The response is returned to the original group or pair and the results are reviewed.

The second group can pass their work to a third group, which then does some further work. If appropriate, this can continue to a fourth group, *etc.* To ensure that no group repeats a paper, this passing can be done cyclically. Once the paper is returned to its original group, there should be time for the group to review it briefly. For some problems, a class-wide follow-up discussion may be valuable.

Both the examples and the solutions are indicative of the quality of understanding. It can be valuable for the instructor to collect and review them. These may be returned with feedback or they may be evaluated for grades. Particularly instructive examples may be shared with the entire class or may be included in a future exam or quiz.

It is not uncommon for a group to ask, "We think the work of the previous group is incorrect. Should we correct it, or just work with their incorrect solution?" Either response may be appropriate, depending on the problem. The group could be asked to write briefly on the paper why they think the previous work is incorrect.

Typical Uses

- Reinforce concepts.

- Explore a variety of mathematical examples.

- Learn to read the work of peers with a critical eye.

Process Skills

In a Group or Pair Exchange, the initial group must reach consensus on the meaning and goal of the problem, then must carry out the instructions and agree on the result. After the papers are exchanged, a group must be able to interpret and work with the results from the previous group. This can present situations different from standard textbook problems. The group may also see new ways of understanding or approaching a problem.

Examples for Groups/Pairs Exchange

- Mathematics for Elementary Education

    – Symmetry: Draw the logo from your automobile. Pass your paper on to another group. Find the symmetries of the figure you receive.

    – Other Bases: Create an addition problem involving a pair of two-digit numbers; do not solve it! Then convert these addends to base 2. Pass your paper to another group. Do the computation in the new base and convert the answer to base 10.

Classroom Strategies

- Elementary Statistics

  – Hypothesis Testing: A certain experiment is designed to decide some specified question. The first group writes the null and alternative hypotheses. The second group writes the meaning of a Type I and a Type II error.

  – Chi Square Testing: (Give one group the hypotheses and observed counts for a 2×2 table.) Find the marginal distribution; pass to another group. Calculate the expected counts; pass to another group. Use your calculator to find the χ^2 value and the p-value. Return to the original group. Review this work and draw a conclusion.

- Discrete Mathematics

  – Propositional Calculus: Write a Boolean expression using at least three variables. Pass your paper on to another group. Create the truth table for the expression you receive.

  – Onto Functions: Read the definition in the text and write a sentence or two explaining what "onto" means. Pass your paper to another group. On the paper you receive, write an example of a function that is not onto, and explain why not. Pass the paper to a third group. On the paper you receive write a definition of "onto" in mathematical notation. Return the paper to its original group.

- Precalculus

  – Linear Equations: Write an equation for a line that passes through the point $(1, 3)$. Pass your paper to another group. Find an equation for the line through $(-1, 3)$ that is perpendicular to the first line. Pass your paper to a third group. Find the intersection point of the two lines.

  – Exponential Functions: The first group creates a story related to exponential growth or decay and writes an exponential function that models their story. The second group comments on the story, then finds the initial "population" and when that population has doubled or halved.

- Calculus

  – Product Rule: Create two functions, one which requires the product rule to differentiate it and one which contains a product but does not require the product rule. Do not do the differentiation! Pass your paper to another group. Calculate the derivatives of the two functions you receive.

  – Integration Methods: Make up a function that requires a trigonometric substitution to integrate it. Do not write down the substitution you chose! Pass your paper to another group. Calculate the antiderivative of the function you receive.

- Linear Algebra

  – Linear Transformations: Make up a 3×3 matrix. (The instructor should state some parameters, to prevent simplistic answers such as the identity matrix.) Pass your paper to another group. Decide if this matrix represents a one-to-one transformation; explain your reasoning. Return the paper; check the answer.

  – Linear Transformations: A certain linear transformation A from $\mathbf{R}^3$ to $\mathbf{R}^2$ has the line $y = 2x$ as its image. Find a possible matrix for A, one with no 0 entries. Pass your paper to a second group. Check the answer, and then find the rank and nullity of A. Pass the paper to a third group. Check the work so far, then find a value b so that the equation $AX = [-5, b]'$ is solvable. Pass the paper to a fourth group. Check the work so far, and then decide how many solutions for X are possible with the given value of b. Return the paper to its original group. Check the work.

- Advanced Topics

  – Abstract Algebra: Find an example of a non-Abelian group. Share your example with another group; are your examples isomorphic or not? How do you know?

  – Abstract Algebra: Find a normal subgroup of the group S_3 (or perhaps S_4) of all permutations of 3 (or 4) objects. Pass your paper to another group. Construct and identify the quotient group. Pass to a third group. Construct a homomorphism of S_3 onto the identified quotient whose kernel is the original normal subgroup.

– Topology: Create an "interesting" subset of a given topological space. Pass to another group. Find the set of all its limit points.

– Game Theory: Construct a 2×2 zero-sum matrix game. Then solve it for the Row Player's optimal strategy. Pass your paper to another group. Solve for the Column Player's optimal strategy.

Group Critique

Description

This is a variation of Groups/Pairs Exchange in which the groups monitor and correct each other's work. The class is given a task or problem to be worked in their groups. After an appropriate amount of time, each group passes its work to another group, which critiques their work. The paper is then returned to the original group.

The paper could be passed to a third or even fourth group before returning it to the owners (reminiscent of Roundtable). This would allow several viewpoints and opinions to accumulate.

All groups could work the same problem or each group could have its own. In the latter case, several groups could present their work to the class. One way to do this is to have each group write their work on an overhead transparency. Rather than passing their work on to another group, each group would present its work for the entire class. This gives an opportunity for the instructor, and the other students, to ask questions or to give feedback that is less personal (and less threatening).

It may be necessary to explain to students the idea of constructive criticism. Reading or posting examples of particularly helpful critiques helps convey what is expected.

Some instructors may feel that they should monitor the students' feedback. Collecting and reviewing the papers is one way to do this. Another approach is to have a group present to the class another group's work and their critique of it, though this has the danger of embarrassing the other group.

Typical Uses

- Practice basic skills.
- Review terminology.
- Construct and evaluate proofs.
- Explain concepts and interpret others' work.
- See other approaches to a problem.

Process Skills

Beyond the behaviors needed for doing the initial work, the second phase of Group Critique asks students to read critically the work of others. They must then respond clearly and constructively to this work. Once the paper is returned, the students must be able to accept criticism from their peers and use it to continue working toward the solution of the problem.

Examples for Group Critique

- Mathematics for Elementary Education

    – Negative Numbers: Explain what -5 means. Write this on a sheet of paper, and write your group name on the paper. Pass to another group. Examine the paper you receive; do you agree with what it says? If your explanation was different, add it to the paper. Return to the original group.

    – Polyhedra: (Each group is given a model of a polyhedron.) Write down everything you can about this object. Refer to your text and give the most precise name you can for your object. Pass your object and your paper to another group; check the description you receive and add anything you can. Return to the original group.

- Elementary Statistics

    – Probability: Each group is given one standard die and one tetrahedral die (numbered 1 to 4). The experiment is to roll both dice and record X = the value on the tetrahedron minus the value on the cube. Find the probability distribution of X and display it in a histogram. Pass to another group. Examine the paper you receive; do you agree with it? Write your comments and return it to the original group.

– Confidence Intervals: Here are excerpts from a recent newspaper article (on an opinion poll). Read these excerpts and answer questions such as:

What population is being surveyed?

What is the sample size?

What is the confidence level?

What is the point estimate for the proportion?

How many people in the sample agree with (a given position)?

What is the standard deviation?

What is the margin of error?

Pass to another group. Examine the paper you receive; do you agree with it? Add your comments and return to the original group.

• Discrete Mathematics

– Relations: Give an example of a relation that is both reflexive and symmetric. Pass your paper to another group; review and correct the paper you receive. A similar problem: Give an example of a relation that is transitive but not symmetric.

– Mathematical Induction: Prove that every third Fibonacci number is even. Pass your paper to another group. Critique the proof you receive.

• Precalculus

– Rational Functions: Create an expression for a function with one vertical asymptote and with two x-intercepts. Pass to another group; review and correct the paper you receive.

– Linear Functions: Write an equation for a line that does not pass through the third quadrant or through the origin. Pass to another group; review and correct the paper you receive. Note: This can also be asked for circles, parabolas, *etc.*

• Calculus

– Derivatives: Using the definition of the derivative, calculate $f'(1)$ for the function

$$f(t) = \begin{cases} t^2 & \text{for } t < 1 \\ 2t & \text{for } t \geq 1 \end{cases}$$

Pass your work to another group. Review

and correct the paper you receive.

– Riemann Sums: For a specified function and interval, draw a diagram of a Riemann sum using n subintervals (with n chosen to produce reasonable values if a uniform partition is used). Pass to another group. Review the diagram you receive; if possible, tell what kind of Riemann sum is represented.

• Linear Algebra

– Dot Product: The dot product $X \cdot Y = x_1 y_1 + x_2 y_2 = |x| |y| \cos \theta$. Write an explanation of the notation in this statement. Pass your paper to another group. Review and correct the paper you receive.

– Proof: Read the proof of Theorem *xx* on page *yy* of the text. Write a paragraph explaining this proof, using only words, *i.e.,* no symbols. Pass your paper to another group. Review and correct the paper you receive.

• Advanced Topics

– In any course with a proof component, it is valuable to have groups first construct a proof, then critique another group's proof.

– In a course that includes applications, such as Mathematical Modeling, Differential Equations, or Operations Research, groups can review the mathematical models developed by other groups.

– Analysis: Fold a sheet of paper into fourths. In three of the sections write definitions of monotone increasing sequence, monotone decreasing sequence, oscillating sequence. Pass to another group; review the paper you receive and make any necessary corrections, explaining why. In each section give an example, and in the fourth section give a "none of the above" example. Return the paper to the original group. A similar activity would examine bounded above, bounded below, and bounded. After doing both of these activities, the groups could classify their examples as convergent or divergent, and then write these on the board. The class could look for conjectures on when an infinite sequence converges.

Triptych

Description

This is a variation of Groups/Pairs Exchange that is particularly effective for studying a process and its reversal. Each group folds a sheet of paper into thirds, as if to put it into an envelope. In the top third, the group performs some task. The sheet is passed to a second group, which performs a task based on the result shown in the top section and writes its result in the middle section. The top third of the paper is folded back to conceal the first result and the sheet is passed to a third group. This group performs a task based on the second result, and records its work in the bottom section. Then the sheet is returned to the original group, which compares the results in the top and bottom sections. This can lead to spirited conversation when the original group sees the third result.

One possible problem with this strategy is that groups may work at different rates or the examples created may be of varying levels of difficulty. Thus there can be timing difficulties in passing the papers. To circumvent this problem, it may be useful to have the groups engaged in some other activity whenever they are not working on the triptych.

The name "Triptych" was first used in March 1996 by J. Lyn Miller of Western Kentucky University in a presentation at the Kentucky Section meeting of the MAA.

Typical Uses

- Study a reversible process, such as differentiation.
- Practice basic skills.
- Explain and compare concepts.
- Recognize common errors.

Process Skills

In the second and third phases of a Triptych, the groups must read and interpret the work of the previous groups. They must then build on this earlier work and reach consensus. Once the paper is returned, the original group must reconcile the final result with the initial one.

Examples for Triptych

- Mathematics for Elementary Education

  – Other Bases: Write a three-digit natural number. Convert this number to base 5 (2, 8, *etc.*) notation. Convert this number back to base 10 notation. Note: This can also be done with Roman or Egyptian numerals.

  – Understanding Multiplication: Write a multiplication problem involving fractions. Draw a diagram to represent this multiplication problem. Write the problem represented by the diagram.

- Elementary Statistics

  – Boxplots: Given a short list of data (perhaps unique to that group) calculate the median, quartiles, and extreme values. Create a boxplot based on these results. Examine the boxplot and determine the median, quartiles, and extreme values.

  – Hypothesis Testing: Given an alternative hypothesis, state the null hypothesis. Draw an appropriate distribution and mark the rejection region. Examine the graph and determine the two hypotheses. Note: If there are various types of distributions involved, say at a review session, each group can present the results at the end.

- Discrete Mathematics

  – Venn Diagrams: Draw a Venn diagram of three sets A, B, and C and mark one of the regions. Write a set description of this region in terms of A, B, C. Draw a Venn diagram and mark the region matching the description.

  – Boolean Functions: Create a Boolean expression using three variables. Find the truth table for this function. Construct a Boolean expression matching the truth table. Follow-up question: If the two expressions are not identical, are they equivalent?

- Precalculus

  – Inverse functions: Sketch the graph of a function of the group's choice. Select an appropriate domain and sketch the inverse of this function. Sketch the inverse of this inverse.

– Polynomial Functions: Create a polynomial function with a specified number of real roots. Find the roots of the given function. Find a polynomial function with the stated roots. A similar problem for rational functions could ask for a function with both a vertical and a horizontal asymptote, and proceed accordingly.

- Calculus

– Derivatives and Antiderivatives: Choose a function, of the group's own devising or from a provided list, and write this in the top section of the paper. Calculate the derivative of this function and write the result in the middle section of the paper. Calculate the antiderivative; in some cases the group may not be able to do so and should try to explain why.

– Graphical Derivatives: Sketch a reasonably interesting function. Sketch the derivative of the function. Reconstruct the original function. Note: This often leads to spirited discussion when the original group sees their reconstructed function. To avoid confusion, it may be useful to agree from the outset that the original function will contain some given point, like $(0, 0)$.

- Linear Algebra

– Different Bases: Write a vector in $\mathbf{R}^2$ (perhaps requiring non-zero entries or different entries). Convert this vector to the basis given by $Q_1 = [3, 4]'$, $Q_2 = [-1, 2]'$, *i.e.,* write the coordinate vector in the new basis. Convert the result of the second step to the standard basis.

- Advanced Topics

– Projective Geometry: Given a statement (axiom or theorem) in projective geometry, draw a diagram illustrating it. State the dual of the statement and draw a diagram illustrating this dual. State the dual of the second statement and draw a diagram. Note: Instead of a diagram, the instructor could ask for a proof. This will require more time, and it may not fit in the limited space on the paper.

– Linear Programming: Given a linear program, solve it (on other paper or with a computer), and write the optimal solution on the paper. Write the dual of the linear program in the second part of the paper, solve it, and write the optimal solution on the paper. Write the dual of the second linear program in the third part of the paper, solve it, and write the optimal solution on the paper.

Pairs-Check

Description

Students work in pairs within groups of four. Each student in a pair plays one of two roles: Solver or Coach. A set of problems on a particular topic or skill is provided to each group. The Solver in each pair works on a problem while the Coach observes carefully, giving hints, pointing out errors as needed, and giving positive feedback to the Solver. Partners switch roles for the second problem in the set. Within the group of four, the pairs check each other's solutions to the first two problems to see if they agree. When both pairs agree, they move on to the next pair of problems.

To use Pairs-Check as an assessment tool, the instructor can collect any subset of the completed problems. The work of individual pairs should indicate who acted as Solver and who acted as Coach for each problem. When the pairs within a group get different results, the group might be asked to explain how they resolved these differences to come up with a group result.

An instructor faces several decisions before implementing Pairs-Check. Should the problems in each pair be of comparable difficulty? Should the first Solver get a choice of problems? There may be something for the student to learn in allowing a choice, for example, recognizing which integration technique to apply. What should be done with a group having an odd number of members? There is also the reality that the groups probably will not finish together, so something must be planned for the quicker groups to do while they wait. A pair of weaker students can cause a significant delay, and such a pair may need some help from the instructor.

Typical Uses

- Practice or master a skill or procedure.
- Review before an examination.

Process Skills

In Pairs-Check, the Solver must learn to work openly without fear of embarrassment. The Coach must listen carefully, watching for errors, and must be open to new approaches to the problem. Further, the Coach must be able to criticize constructively and the Solver must be able to accept this criticism. The fact that the roles reverse for the second problem may encourage these behaviors.

Examples for Pairs-Check

- Mathematics for Elementary Education

  – Decimals and Rationals: Write $0.5\overline{9}$ as a fraction; write $1.4\overline{8}$ as a fraction; *etc.*

  – Other Bases: One student rolls a pair of standard dice and computes the sum (or product) in base 7; the other student checks the result. Each problem and solution is recorded; after doing several problems, the pairs exchange papers and check the work of the other group.

- Elementary Statistics

  – Probability: (Each group is given one standard die and one tetrahedral die, numbered 1 to 4. They perform some experiments to become familiar with the sample space.) Find the probability of rolling doubles. Find the probability that 4 is the larger value.

  – Hypothesis Testing: Suppose the null hypothesis is H_0: My parachute is packed correctly. Explain what a Type I error would mean in this situation. Explain what a Type II error would mean. Similar question: Let H_0 be: This patient needs heart surgery.

- Discrete Mathematics

  – Other Bases: Convert 1101_2 to base 10. Convert 0.101_2 to base 10. Convert 451_8 to base 10. Convert 451_8 to base 2, *etc.*

  – Propositional Calculus: Complete the truth table for $\neg(A \wedge B)$. Complete the truth table for $\neg A \wedge \neg B$. Complete the truth table for $\neg(A \vee B)$. Complete the truth table for $\neg A \vee \neg B$. Compare your results and draw a conclusion.

- College Algebra or Precalculus

  – Algebraic Skills: Each Solver simplifies an algebraic expression from a worksheet provided by the instructor.

  – Laws of Sines and Cosines: A worksheet with diagrams of triangles is provided for which the lengths of some of the sides and the measures of some of the angles are provided. Each Solver finds all of the missing measurements for each triangle.

- Calculus

  – Chain Rule: Each Solver finds an expression for the derivative of $\cos(x^2 + 1)$. The problem set continues with variations of $\cos(g(x))$ where $g(x)$ takes on various forms.

  – Integration by Parts: Each Solver finds $\int x \sin x\, dx$. The problem set continues with additional problems requiring integration by parts.

- Linear Algebra

  – Matrix Multiplication: For a given pair of 3×3 matrices A and B, the first student computes the product AB. The second student computes BA. They compare results.

  – Inverse of a Matrix: Given a 3×3 matrix A, form the augmented matrix $[A \mid I]$ and reduce it to find A^{-1}. The first student is given a matrix of rank 3, the second one of rank 2. Follow-up question to the group: How do you explain what happened?

- Advanced Topics

  – Abstract Algebra: Construct operation tables for all groups of order 3. Do the same for all groups of order 4.

– Topology: Formulate a definition of continuity in terms of open sets. Formulate a definition of continuity in terms of neighborhoods. Show that the first definition implies the second. Prove the reverse implication.

Three-Step Interviews

Description

A group of four students divides into two pairs. Each pair contains an Interviewer and a Speaker. After conducting an interview, the partners switch roles. Finally, the students report to the group what they have learned from their partners. Equal time is given for the first and second interviews, the amount depending on the topic.

If this strategy is used before formal groups have been established, the pairs can conduct their interviews and then report to the class as a whole.

Students may need to be coached on how to interview effectively, that is, how to listen actively by asking clarifying questions and paraphrasing what is heard without taking over the conversation or interjecting their own opinions. The instructor could assign the topics during the preceding class period to give students time to think of questions and responses before the interviews take place.

Typical Uses

• Begin to get to know other students at the beginning of a course.

• Determine the general level of understanding of a particular topic.

• Help students personalize more abstract mathematical concepts.

• Generate multiple examples or approaches.

Process Skills

The major burden is on the Interviewer. This student must ask effective questions and actively listen to the responses. Further, the Interviewer must be able to encourage a reticent Speaker to respond. The sharing at each stage of this strategy promotes a sense of team involvement.

Examples for Three-Step Interviews

• General

– Introductions: Students interview each other using questions such as: How would you describe yourself (hometown, hobbies, favorite sports, movies, food, music, and so on)? Why are you enrolled in this course? What do you hope to gain from the course? What have been your most memorable experiences with mathematics, both positive and negative?

– Group Dynamics: What do you feel is going well in our group? What would you like to improve? How could this improvement take place?

– Problem Solving: (Given a particular problem.) What would you do first in working this problem? What is the next step? *Etc.* What sort of answer would you expect at the end?

• Mathematics for Elementary Education

– Students interview each other about examples of particular geometric figures in their local environment.

• Precalculus

– Students interview each other about situations around town where trigonometry could be employed to measure a particular length or angle.

• Calculus

– Students interview each other about examples of rates of change (or of accumulations) that they encounter in daily life.

Send-a-Problem

Description

Each student makes up a question on a given topic and writes it on a card or sheet of paper. The other students in the group attempt to answer the question. Once a consensus is reached, the answer is written on the back. The group's set of questions is passed to another group, which attempts to answer them. Their answers are then compared to the ones on the backs of the sheets.

For more sophisticated topics, each group could write a question and send it to another group. The second group then decides on an answer, writes it on the back, and returns the card to the original group. This group then has to decide whether the answer is correct.

To share problems beyond the two groups described above, groups could present one or two of the problems to the class, using either the board or a transparency. The sets of questions could circulate to several groups; this will, of course, be time-consuming. The instructor could collect all questions, shuffle them, and pass them out again.

If a question or its answer is ambiguous or unclear, this could be noted on the sheet of paper. Once the sheet is returned to its owners, they could be asked to clarify their work.

Typical Uses

- Practice skills.
- Review terminology.
- Review before an exam.

Process Skills

Either individually or as a group, the students learn to compose problems that are appropriate for the topics and level of the course. When solving these problems and when comparing solutions, students must interpret the work of others. As a group, they must be able to reach consensus on a solution.

Examples for Send-a-Problem

The questions posed when using this strategy are constructed by the students in the class. The instructor can specify the topic or the type of question or can provide a list of topics from which to choose.

When using Send-A-Problem as review before a test, the instructor could indicate the topics to be covered by the test or that the test will cover a particular unit or chapter. The students might be reminded that, when reviewing for an upcoming test, it is often helpful to construct questions that would be appropriate for the test and then try to answer them.

Here is how Bill Fenton conducted a review session for Linear Algebra in Spring 1999. He wrote important concepts from the semester, such as column space and inverse of a matrix, on index cards, with slightly more concepts than the number of students in the class. One week before the final class day, each student drew a card at random and was assigned to write a problem using that concept. With a few extra cards, students had the option of trading for a new randomly chosen card (but only once!). On the final day, the cards were collected, shuffled, and passed out to the groups. The groups solved the problems they received. They selected the problem that they felt was most difficult and wrote it, with its solution, on the blackboard. The class then reviewed the problems displayed on the board.

Jigsaw

Description

As its title suggests, the Jigsaw strategy consists of cutting a task into pieces, which are studied separately and then re-assembled. Here are two common ways to do this.

Students initially are in Home groups. A problem with multiple components is posed to the class. To examine these different components, Expert groups are formed, each of which contains exactly one student from each Home group. Each Expert group addresses one of the components of the problem. After the Expert groups have completed their work, the students return to their Home groups, where each one teaches the other members the portion he has learned.

A simpler method for Jigsaw is to have each existing group investigate one portion, aspect, or approach to a problem or topic. The results are shared with the class, either to prepare for further work or to suggest a general conjecture. This investigation could take place in or out of class, depending on the scope of the work.

Both of these methods are represented in the examples below.

If Expert groups end up with seven or more members, it may be better to divide them into smaller subgroups. An additional concern when Jigsaw is done during class time is that some groups, Expert or Home, may finish before others. Perhaps some additional task should be posed for these groups to do.

It is important that the students be held accountable for the material presented by their peers. For instance, this material could be included on a test. A danger, of course, is that an inferior presentation may put some students at a disadvantage. If the students are told in advance that this material will be tested, it may spur greater efforts by the presenters. Further, the students receiving the presentations may become more demanding in their questions. The instructor must also decide whether to supplement an incomplete presentation, perhaps at a later class period.

Typical Uses

- Examine large or multifaceted issues.

- Solve a large set of preliminary problems before reaching the main problem.

- Consider various cases in the proof of a theorem.

- Investigate different strategies for solving the same problem.

- Develop or extend an important topic in the course through group projects.

- Learn about a large body of material by receiving presentations from experts.

- Study a topic that is not presented in the normal progress of the course.

Process Skills

The Expert groups often must read and interpret material that has not been presented in class. They must agree on the solution of their problem or the important aspects of their research. In Home groups, each individual must act as peer teacher, requiring that person to give a focused and meaningful report. Students must be active listeners and must ask insightful questions, for they will be accountable for this material later.

Examples for Jigsaw

- General

  – The Jigsaw strategy can be used for completing course readings outside of class: here the Expert groups would closely study some part of the readings, then the students would return to their Home groups to share what they had learned with their other Home group members.

  – Jigsaw also can be used to include a topic in a course that has not been covered by the text. The instructor could develop a series of separate assignments that build on each other and assign one topic to each group. Each group researches its topic and prepares a report for the whole class. These reports could be spread throughout the term. For example, if the topic is graph theory, different groups might research and report on such topics as (1) What is a Graph? , (2) Coloring a Graph, (3) Circuits and Paths in Graphs, and (4) Using Graphs to Solve a Puzzle Like Instant Insanity. If the topics build on each other, students will realize that they need to know the material in earlier presentations in order to do their own research for a later presentation. This helps to promote individual accountability and helps to create an atmosphere in which everyone is really listening to the reports and asking penetrating questions.

- Mathematics for Elementary Education

  – Subtraction: Three Expert groups explain and create examples for the three standard interpretations of subtraction: Take-Away, Comparison, Missing Addend. Then the Home groups discuss and compare the interpretations.

  – Polya's Problem-Solving Scheme: The Polya Scheme has four steps. Each group can discuss one of the steps and be prepared to explain what it means to the class. Alternatively, Expert groups can discuss the four steps separately, and then the Home groups can review the steps and perhaps apply them to a specific problem.

- Elementary Statistics

  – Binomial Distributions: Consider the experiment of flipping a coin n times and recording the number X of heads. In a class with n groups, each group calculates one of the probabilities that $X = 0, X = 1, \ldots, X = n$. The class then creates a histogram of this distribution. Possible follow-up question: Consider an unbalanced coin with $p = \frac{2}{3}$. Recalculate these probabilities and draw the new histogram. Compare to the earlier work.

– Preliminary to ANOVA: Each group is given a handout with data and is assigned one of the factors (with perhaps some repeats). The group finds $\bar{x}$, s, n, and a 90% confidence interval for μ for its designated factor and writes its results on the board. Follow-up question: Could the population means be equal?

- Discrete Mathematics

– Complete Graphs: Each of the N groups is assigned a value j from 1 to N. Group j then draws a graph having j vertices and as many edges as possible, and counts the edges. The results are recorded on the board and the class attempts to find a general formula for the number of edges in K_n.

– Trees: Here are four characterizations of a tree: (a) a connected graph with no circuits; (b) a graph having a unique path between any two vertices; (c) a connected graph having n vertices and $n-1$ edges; (d) a minimal connected graph on n vertices. Each (existing or Expert) group is assigned one component of the proof that these are equivalent, namely (a) implies (b), (b) implies (c), (c) implies (d), or (d) implies (a).

- Precalculus

– Transformations on graphs: Expert groups examine the effects of various transformations applied to the sine function. Home groups then combine this expertise to produce a graph of a new function.

– Simultaneous Linear Equations: Each group is given a different set of equations and asked to solve their system both graphically and algebraically. (The sets should represent all possible cases.) Then a few groups can present their results, making sure that all cases are included.

- Calculus

– Average Rates: Suppose $f(t) = 16t^2$ represents the distance in feet an object has fallen in t seconds. Starting at 2 seconds, what is the average rate of this object in the next 1, 0.1, 0.01, 0.001, ... seconds? Each group is assigned a different number of seconds. The results are put in a table and the class is asked what happens as the time interval approaches 0.

– Function Notation: Explain what $f(a)$ means and how to evaluate it when the function f is represented by an expression, a set of ordered pairs, a graph, or a tuple. Expert groups each examine one type of representation, then report to their Home groups. Another method is to have each existing group prepare one response and then have a cross section of groups present their explanations.

- Linear Algebra

– Vector Spaces: Here is a set of vectors: $\{a + bx \mid a, b \in \mathbf{R}\}$. Each group is assigned two or more of the vector space properties to verify. Note: It may be valuable to have some properties assigned to more than one group, to check the work and perhaps find alternative proofs.

– Eigenspaces: Given a matrix and its eigenvalues, each group finds the eigenspace of a designated eigenvalue. Note: The particular matrix to use may depend on whether the students have access to technology for this work. If there are more groups than eigenvalues, two or more groups could work on each value and then exchange papers to check their work.

- Advanced Topics

– Regular Polyhedra: After the class has discussed Euler's Formula, each group is assigned one regular polygon (triangle, square, and so on) and asked to decide if this shape could be used to create a regular polyhedron.

– Lagrange's Theorem: Given Lagrange's Theorem, Expert groups separately consider the partition lemma, the cardinality lemma, the proof of the theorem using these lemmas, and an application to finding all groups of a given (prime) order. Home groups then apply Lagrange's Theorem to find all groups of order 6.

– Sensitivity Analysis for Linear Programming: For a given solved linear program, Expert groups consider how to update the solution when: the objective function is changed; the resources are changed; some constraints are changed; a new constraint is added. The individual experts then present their knowledge to their Home groups.

Choosing an Appropriate Cooperative Strategy

Experienced teachers have clear goals for their course and curriculum. Curriculum goals include both content objectives and process objectives. For most college or university courses, the content goals are usually clear. For example, after completing Calculus a student is generally expected to be able to compute derivatives and to be able to apply the results of such calculations appropriately. However, process goals are frequently less clear. In mathematics courses, we want our students to learn to gather facts and data, to explore an idea or concept, to read about a concept and make valid interpretations, and to be able to explain their ideas or their results both orally and in writing. We expect them to be able to apply what they have learned to solve new problems and to extend what they understand in one area to other related areas. We want them to be able to write clear mathematical proofs. Many of these skills serve our students well in all spheres of learning, not just in mathematics. Further, we hope that our seniors have acquired a certain mathematical maturity—an ability to solve problems using things they have learned over several semesters—and an insight into mathematical ideas at a deeper level. It is not always clear in just which course we expect the students to acquire this depth of insight or mathematical sophistication; we may become aware of our expectations only when our seniors fail to meet them. Many of these unmet expectations may be unstated process goals of the curriculum.

Group tasks can be formulated that support both content and process goals. The instructor should establish precisely the goals that he wants to accomplish. Activities then can be planned to develop an understanding of the relevant mathematical concepts and, at the same time, develop

these broader skills. Groups can be used to have students check each other's work for mistakes, to help clarify a concept by having students explain it to each other, or to gather and share data. Group work can compel written or verbal communication and student interaction, and it can challenge students to search for resources. Conferring with group members can facilitate the use of technology. A new concept might be introduced through group work on discovery and exploration activities. Groups can be assigned longer projects that are too much work for one person. In these and many other ways, groups of students working together on problems can be used to encourage and enhance the learning of individual students.

The nature of the lesson may suggest a particular strategy. Does the activity need to be reported to the class or will the work within the groups suffice? Will there be follow-up discussion? Do the students have the resourcefulness and initiative to work independently within their groups? Is the class too large to allow extensive reporting from the groups? Is it too small to generate contrasting views? These and similar issues can influence the instructor's choice of cooperative strategy.

Let us simplify a bit and organize these curricular goals into four broad categories—facts, skills, concepts, and applications.

- **Facts:** Many mathematics problems require data: data to be analyzed, data to complete a computation, or data to use as a foundation for conceptual understanding. Students should be able to recognize the sort of data needed, and then to collect or derive it. They should be able to search for examples or counterexamples for a conjecture.

- **Skills:** Students must develop proficiency with mechanics such as factoring, simplifying, and differentiating. Communicating mathematical ideas covers a wide range of important skills: reading mathematics, interpreting definitions and theorems, explaining ideas both orally and in writing, and listening critically to one another's explanations. Being able to locate and use resources, which today include technology, is vital. Another critical skill is finding errors in one's own work or in another's. And, although some may consider proof an art, there are skills involved in writing clear proofs.

- **Concepts:** Students must look for patterns and generalities. It can be difficult to see the common thread joining a set of examples, even when the connection is explained by the instructor or the text, and students need practice with moving from the specific to the general. Students should learn to speculate, then to confirm (prove) or refute their conjectures. Moving from the general to the specific can also be a challenge; to many students it is by no means obvious how to interpret a mathematical statement such as a theorem in a particular situation.

- **Applications:** Students should be able to solve new problems. To do so, they must learn to recognize which components are essential and which are irrelevant. The problems could relate directly to the mathematics being studied or could tie together several topics. The problems could ask the students to extend concepts to new areas. Students should see how mathematics is used to solve problems in other disciplines.

While a particular cooperative strategy may fit some of these categories more naturally than the others, any of the strategies discussed in this chapter can be used for many purposes. Their use is limited only by the creativity of the instructor. In addition, the instructor may find that each class of students will respond somewhat differently to a given strategy. Like all teaching, choosing an appropriate classroom strategy requires practice and improves with experience.

Creating Your Own Cooperative Strategies

The set of strategies in this chapter offers a wide selection of approaches for classroom activities. Many strategies can be varied easily to fit the needs of a particular topic or problem. Yet experienced instructors may wish to try their own ideas for creating a cooperative learning situation. We encourage you to experiment. (If something works especially well, please let us know about it. We are always looking for new strategies.)

Two fundamental principles of cooperative learning are team reward and individual accountability. These are particularly important when designing a cooperative activity. The goal is to have students working together to learn, with responsibility not just for themselves but for their groupmates as well. The strategy should be structured to encourage contributions from everyone in the group. Everyone must feel both a pressure to contribute and a need for other's contributions, so that they achieve both individual benefit and group benefit.

For larger projects, which have a substantial impact on the grading scheme, the scoring ideally should allow students at all levels to make a meaningful contribution to the group effort. For instance, a project that includes a presentation to the class might require both a written and an oral report, and perhaps the in-class portion would be supported by multimedia. These additional components can give group members an opportunity to contribute expertise outside the mathematics of the project. Furthermore, preparing these presentations would give these students a deeper experience with the mathematics.

Designing and Adapting Good Group Problems

Good problems engage most of the students most of the time, engaging them in problem solving and in thinking about mathematics in a serious way. The main goals are to give students a chance to participate more actively and to force them to enter into a discussion of the concepts, of the given information, and of the approaches to use. A good group problem should challenge students and should expose them to a variety of approaches to solving any particular problem. Certain types of problems can reinforce process skills, and some problems can be structured to bring out the expertise and unique contributions of each individual.

Groups can work on problems that are more complex, beyond the reach of the typical individual. On the other hand, group problems do not need to be the most challenging ones. As students learn to work cooperatively, some problems can be posed which individuals may be able to solve individually. Early in the term, students usually will not attempt to interact unless it is necessary, and activities should be structured to force this interaction. But after a group learns the value of sharing its ideas and expertise, its discussion occurs naturally even for less daunting problems. When working together students often develop alternative approaches to problems and will recognize that these are equally valid. This helps to break down the stereotype that the only proper solution strategy is the one demonstrated by the instructor. Here are some general categories of problems that lend themselves to group work.

Problems that can be solved in more than one way

For example, given two quantities (such as size of two populations, manufacturing cost and revenue generated, or profits for two different corporations), the question can be: When will these two quantities become equal? Different groups can be asked to pursue graphical, tabular, or analytic solutions, or left to devise their own method. Afterwards, in a discussion with the whole class, students can share their strategies, compare their results, and decide which method was superior. Problems like this often are ideal for a Jigsaw strategy.

Problems having multiple correct answers

In Precalculus, students might be asked to consider cubic polynomials, and to (a) identify two distinct properties that such a function *must* exhibit; (b) identify two distinct properties that it *might* exhibit; and then (c) give two examples of cubics that, respectively, do and do not exhibit one of the properties they listed in (b). Here a brainstorming strategy such as Roundtable can work well.

Problems that lead to follow-up questions or to more sophisticated topics

For example, when exploring the connection between the factored form of a polynomial function and the intercepts of its graph, groups might be asked to find a quadratic function that correctly models a map of a "hilltop" when only the two *x*-intercepts are specified. A follow-up problem would be to specify the height of the hill as well. The Think-Pair-Share or Numbered-Heads-Reporting strategies often are good for a sequence of related problems.

Problems that include a variety of operations which can be divided among the members of the group

To introduce students to the concepts of linear functions and proportionality, the class can go into a physics laboratory. Each group gets a set of masses to hang on a spring mounted vertically next to a meter stick, and the group gathers and plots data of spring extension versus mass added. The group then tries to fit a line to those data. Ideally, different members of each group will take charge of hanging the masses, tabulating the data, drawing the graph, and fitting a line to it.

Problems with some not-immediately-obvious feature

Suppose college algebra students are being asked to characterize some polynomials according to their roots, extrema, asymptotic behavior, and so on. It is good to include examples that have two roots very close together, that have interesting behavior outside the standard viewing window of the students' graphing calculators, *etc.* Such quirks are often overlooked by the quicker workers of the group and noticed by someone who is more attentive and meticulous, but perhaps a bit slower. This phenomenon helps the group members appreciate the different skills that each one brings to the group. (This presumes that students are appropriately placed in the course.)

Another possibility is to pose a problem that is missing some necessary information. In this case the instructor should wait until asked to provide it or should expect the students to find it independently. An example from physics (introductory mechanics) is a variation on standard collision problems. A typical textbook problem supposes two vehicles collide at a given angle and gives the students exactly what they need to know to determine how far and in what direction the resulting wreck slides (assuming the two vehicles remain together). This variation is to tell the students the length and direction of the skid mark, but to omit the value for the coefficient of friction between the tires and the concrete. The students are asked to determine which (if either) of the vehicles was initially exceeding the speed limit. Now the problem is more like an actual court case, and the students have to supply a reasonable value for the missing data and then defend their choice. By pitting groups against each other as teams for the defense and the prosecution, it is possible to explore how far the facts of the case can reasonably be stretched to benefit one side or the other.

Another example of this sort of problem, from Mathematics for Elementary Education, is to ask how many sheets of construction paper are needed to cut out shapes (hearts, shamrocks, or turkeys, for instance) to decorate a bulletin board. The size of the bulletin board, the size and design of the desired shapes, and the size of the construction paper, or reasonable estimates of these data, are needed before the problem can be completed.

Exploration problems

Carefully designed problems or problem sets can be used to present entirely new concepts. To study transformations on quadratic and rational equations, for instance, students can explore many equations using their graphing calculators and carefully constructed worksheets. Starting with familiar equations, each sheet can have them explore one type of transformation via a collection of examples, *e.g.,* $y = x^2 + b$ with varying values of b, $y = (x - c)^2 + b$ with varying values of first c and then both c and b, and so on. After each set of examples, the students write a description of how the transformation affected the graph and write an example of another transformation which had the same sort of effect. These activities can be done in class, outside of class, or some mixture, and they can include open-ended responses. Because this requires calculator work and not all students will key things in correctly, nor will any one student always make the hoped-for generalizations, it works well to have students work in groups and submit only one result.

Review problems

For example, after studying polynomials and the rational zeros theorem, one instructor wanted the students to review what they knew about polynomials. She listed the properties that she wanted the students to review: degree, number of zeros, end-behavior as x approaches infinity and negative infinity, *etc.* She then designed polynomials having all combinations of these, with some polynomials expressed in standard form, some in factored form, and so on. These were presented to the class. The problem sheet generated much good discussion of mathematics: How do you know this polynomial has two real zeros? How do you know it has no complex zeros? How do you know that both ends approach positive infinity? The students needed to coordinate many pieces of information about the polynomials. It proved to be a good culminating

activity, helping the students ascertain what they did not understand and thus what to concentrate on when studying for the test.

The last item in the list above illustrates one way to create group activities: decide on the concept(s) to be presented, design prototypic examples, then direct the student groups to examine the examples, to draw conclusions, and to justify those conclusions. This is a good approach for those just beginning to use group work. Later, as an instructor grows more confident with group work and more aware of various classroom strategies, the activities can become more varied.

It can be an intimidating, even terrifying, prospect to create group activities, particularly for an instructor new to cooperative learning. But it is not necessary to do everything from scratch. Many newer textbooks include group activities, and some are designed specifically for a cooperative learning setting. (A partial list of these appears in the Bibliography.) Good group problems also can be constructed by adapting existing problems. A traditional textbook problem can be modified by broadening the statement, by removing some of the information or assumptions, or in other ways making it more open-ended. Often what had been an unremarkable problem will become an opportunity to explore a wide range of issues and to engage the students deeply.

A closing tip: One way to encourage group interaction is to pass out only one copy of the worksheet or assignment to each group. This forces the group members to share the work, at least at the initial stages. However, a more complex problem probably warrants copies for everyone.

Credits and Acknowledgments

Much of the material in this chapter is based on a workshop Neil Davidson presented for the Washington State Calculus Consortium. The staff of that workshop suggested some of the example questions; later these lists of examples were greatly expanded by participants in MAA Project CLUME Workshops and by the chapter's authors. Several additional strategies, which seem consistent with Davidson's work, have also been included in this set. Davidson's original handout was edited by Janet Ray and later expanded by Barbara Reynolds and Bill Fenton.

Classroom Strategies

Spencer Kagan has developed various cooperative structures including Roundtable, Numbered-Heads Reporting, and Pairs-Check. See Kagan (1992).

Mike Pepe at Seattle Central Community College developed Think-Share-Write as a variation of the Davidson strategy Think-Pair-Share.

The idea for Groups/Pairs Exchange came from a graphical derivatives problem presented in a workshop given by Deborah Hughes Hallett of the Harvard Calculus Consortium.

The idea for One-Minute Papers comes from K. Patricia Cross and Thomas A. Angelo (1988). Jean MacGregor and others have proposed some of the useful and imaginative variations on this strategy.

Summary of Chapter 3

In this chapter we present fifteen cooperative strategies for day-to-day classroom use. The strategies progress from those that can be used fairly easily to others that are more complex. Each comes with a description of how to implement it and a discussion of issues to consider before doing so. Typical uses for the strategy are listed, with a brief discussion of the process skills required or encouraged by this strategy. Each presentation concludes with a set of specific examples chosen from a variety of undergraduate mathematics courses.

The chapter also contains general advice on how to get started with cooperative learning, some brief guidelines for choosing an appropriate strategy to present a specific topic, and suggestions for designing or adapting problems for group work.

Chapter 4

Designing Assessment Activities to Encourage Productive Collaboration

Barbara E. Reynolds, Anthony D. Thomas, Ronald J. Milne

What Makes Collaboration Work?

As teachers, our goal is to increase individual achievement. We want students to have a deeper understanding of the course material, an increased ability to apply concepts and solve problems in new contexts or new situations, and a longer retention of important skills and concepts. In contrast, the (short-term) goal of many undergraduate students is to get a good (individual) grade at the end of the course.

Sometimes a student's strategies for achieving a good course grade seem to undermine the instructor's objective in asking students to cooperate on learning activities. For example, a group of students may work together to complete an assigned task by dividing up the work. If they do not come back together as a group to reflect on how the individual components are related to the solution of the whole problem, they might get a good grade on the assignment without each one learning everything that was needed to complete the assignment. The individual students might not learn as much as if they had done the task individually. That is, working together to complete an assigned task is not necessarily the same as collaborating to learn. One of the challenges that face the instructor who is using cooperative learning is to design tasks in such a way that students really do collaborate to learn.

Cooperative learning is a pedagogical strategy that uses group work and social interaction to increase a student's personal engagement with the course content. Working together on learning tasks provides students with opportunities to articulate or verbalize ideas by asking questions and explaining concepts to each other. Cooperative learning strategies tend to increase individual achievement if there is positive interdependence, individual accountability, assessment that includes group work, and a positive *esprit de corps* among the members of the group. Studies have shown a positive correlation between the number and quality of interactions among the members of a group and the achievement gains of individual members of the group. College and university students can learn to engage in more productive dialog by regularly monitoring their group processing. Let's consider each of these points.

- **Positive interdependence:** The members of the group must cooperate in order to complete the task.

- **Individual accountability:** It is important for individuals to perceive that they cannot ride to success on someone else's work. Each member of the group must be held responsible for learning the course material and achieving the goals of the course. Undergraduate students will typically complain (with good reason) if they perceive that those who are not involved in a full share of the

55

work are rewarded with good grades.

• **Assessment includes group work:** Cooperative learning in undergraduate education is more productive when group work is included directly in the grading process. Since students are working to maximize their individual course grades, they tend to engage in behaviors that are perceived as directly affecting their final course grade.

• **Positive *esprit de corps*:** In groups that have a positive *esprit de corps*, group members feel mutually responsible for each other. They sense that each individual's achievements will help the whole group. Each member of the group realizes he will do better as others in the group do better or get higher grades.

• **Number and quality of interactions:** Studies have shown that giving and receiving explanations is positively correlated with achievement, while receiving terminal answers or no answer at all is negatively related to achievement. (See, for example, Web, 1982; cited in Slavin, 1983b.)

• **Regular monitoring of group processing:** At the end of a class period or work session, students should be given an opportunity to reflect on what they did well, and what they could have done better. This helps students learn how to work together more constructively.

Even if our students accept our arguments that collaboration will improve how much and how well they learn the course material, most students have to perceive that each one's individual grade depends directly on participation in the group activity. Ideally the grade each individual receives reflects some level of individual achievement, but this is not always practical. If the group turns in one product, for example, a group report or presentation, how is the instructor to assign grades that reflect individual understanding or achievement?

Types of Assessment

Assessment can be either formative or summative, or some combination of both. Formative assessments reflect progress toward a goal, and summative assessments reflect how well the student has mastered the material at some point in time, such as by the end of the course. Strictly speaking, course grades should be summative, and formative

assessments should be used to make instructional decisions throughout the course. In a traditional undergraduate lecture-based course, grades are typically based on individual performance on tests, exams, projects, and papers. These measures, which tend to be summative in nature, may also be used in classrooms that use cooperative learning.

Instructors using cooperative learning may employ a variety of additional methods of continuing formative assessments: informal observations during in-class activities, oral or written responses to questions posed in class, and ungraded homework. Students tend to take quizzes, unit/chapter tests, and course assignments more seriously if they perceive that their final course grade is directly affected by their work on these earlier assessments, which are often formative in nature. For this reason, many instructors include quiz grades, class attendance and participation, and grades on chapter/unit tests in the overall grading scheme for the course. By blurring the distinction between formative and summative assessments, many instructors are using a grading scheme that is structured to be both motivational and evaluative.

Cooperative learning depends on group activities that can be used by both instructor and students in assessing understanding of course material. In-class writing activities provide opportunities for students to articulate their understanding of a concept as well as a means for students and their instructors to assess their current level of understanding of the concept. Responses to questions posed during class discussion provide another means of assessing students' understanding, and they help guide the choice of activity for the next step in the instructional process. Ungraded homework is a learning activity that provides an opportunity for formative assessment. Graded homework and quizzes might also be used as formative assessments. Some instructors report that they grade homework and quizzes in order to motivate students to take them more seriously. However, these may contribute only a small percentage to the student's final course grade.

Some of us have also used electronic communication (email) to give students an opportunity to verbalize their current understanding of a concept or topic. Students can be asked to respond by a specified time to a question posed during class discussion. Typically this due date/time is sufficiently before the next class period that the instructor can review students' responses and incorporate these into the next class discussion. For example, for a class meeting on Monday, Wednesday, and Friday, students might be asked to send an email response to the instructor by noon on Sunday.

In our collective experience over many years of teaching, the authors have observed that students who engage in most of the learning activities of the course—including the group work on problems, computer-based activities, and course projects—tend to do better on tests of individual achievement and mastery. These students also tend to be better prepared for subsequent courses. As we have enticed students to engage more seriously in cooperative learning activities, we have found it less necessary to re-teach material covered in the prerequisite courses. So it seems not entirely dishonest or misleading to include formative measures of achievement in the evaluation of each student's mastery of the course material as long as the formative and motivational measures don't weigh too heavily in the evaluation.

What Skills Are Being Assessed

Learning mathematics involves a large set of related skills, only some of which are measured on a traditional in-class test. Our students need to develop a facility with the language of mathematics. That is, they need to be able to read, write, and speak mathematics. A written exam provides an opportunity to assess the student's ability to write mathematics, but tells us little about the student's ability to talk about the same ideas. A test covering only material presented in lectures provides an opportunity to assess listening comprehension while telling us less about the student's reading comprehension.

Students should be able to work on complex problems that are too involved to solve in the timeframe of an in-class test. Group projects provide a setting in which students must talk with their peers about problems. A collaboratively written report challenges students to evaluate each other's statements about a solution to a problem. Writing an individual response to a problem during a timed in-class test does not require this same evaluative process. When students realize that each of them will be evaluated, *i.e.,* graded, on the basis of what is written in the group report, they take ownership of the written work.

Students should be able to use the mathematical tools they are learning in the course to solve a variety of problems. A graded homework set consisting of many problems requiring different problem-solving strategies might assess skills different from skills assessed on an in-class test on a relatively focused subset of problems. When students are asked to work individually on a particular problem set, they can be assessed on skills different from skills assessed when they are expected to work collaboratively.

Inviting Students to Cooperate for Learning

Working with others requires commitment of time and energy. Individuals collaborate if there is some perceived benefit for the effort that is involved. In the workplace, people collaborate effectively if they have a common goal and if they perceive that collaboration is essential (or at least helpful) toward achieving that goal. Why shouldn't our students expect the same?

As educators, how can we design class activities that intrinsically require collaboration? Instead of giving assignments that could be done individually and suggesting that students work together, we need to think of ways to structure class activities so that the motivation to collaborate is built directly into the task itself. If the problem to be solved or the project to be completed is large and complex, there may be incentive for students to collaborate or at least to divide the large task into manageable portions. When students perceive the project as being just beyond their reach as individuals, they want to work together.

However, students have been known to be clever enough to complete a group task while circumventing the actual learning components. If the project is well designed, each student will engage in significant learning activities as the group completes the task. So the challenge facing the instructor who is using cooperative learning is to design group tasks in such a way that if the work is divided among the members of the group significant opportunities for learning are embedded in each component of the overall project.

Course Grades for College/University Students

Most instructors are required by their institutions to evaluate the work of individual students and to give an overall course grade at the end of the term. What elements go into the calculation of such a course grade? What kinds of grading schemes can be used in classrooms that make significant use of cooperative learning groups? In a traditional classroom in which lecture is the dominant pedagogical strategy, a student's grade usually depends on performance on two or three tests and a final exam. Graded homework and a term paper or course project also may be used. In a classroom in which a significant amount of the work of the course has been done in cooperative learning groups, additional assessment may involve journals, class participation, group or individual quizzes, ungraded homework, and group tests.

Among the authors and the survey respondents, journals were used in a variety of ways. Some asked students to keep a daily log of learning activities, those done individually and those done with their group. Others asked the students to write reflections on what they know and what they are learning. Journal writing can be a way of teaching students to be more reflective of their own learning process, and it can be a tool for assessing what each student is learning and what each student is struggling to learn.

Evaluation is a complicated issue. After struggling with evaluation and grading issues over many years, the authors and many of the respondents to our survey report that a variety of alternatives are employed. These fall on a spectrum ranging from most conservative (individual quizzes and tests) to most radical (group grades on group tests, used occasionally and with caution). Some successful cooperative learning practitioners give group grades while others do not. Depending on the instructor's personal style and the rapport among the students in the class, it may not be necessary (most of the time) to grade students for their individual performance in small groups during class. Doing so might lead to competition among students and damage the development of an *esprit de corps*. The grading of group project presentations and reports, typically based on research and group work outside of class, usually requires clear criteria and clear individual accountability.

The accompanying table suggests some of the issues involved with the use of these elements of assessment in a cooperative learning environment. This is an attempt to identify some of the opportunities (benefits) and challenges (possible problems) of each element of assessment, but we have made no effort to be comprehensive.

Assessment Element	Possible benefit in cooperative environment	Possible problem in cooperative environment
Journal	Individual assessment of group work Each student can reflect on both the content and the process of learning	Logistics and students' time involvement Motivation to write entries regularly Time consuming for instructor to appraise
Participation	Motivate active involvement of all	May inflate grades
Homework	Opportunity to work on a broad selection of problems	
Group Task:	Potential to do more complicated tasks Provides rich environment to learn from each other	Tendency to divide up the work Individual's false sense of understanding
Individual Task:	Holds individual responsible	Devalues group dynamics
Quiz, Test, Final Exam Group Part:	Measure of group achievement Provide group rewards	Time taken to organize group's work Conflict over different solutions Does not measure individual achievement
Individual Part:	Measure of individual achievement Assures individual responsibility for learning Group rewards possibly based on individual achievements	Not consistent with learning environment
Group Lab Report	Potential to learn from each other	Possibility of freeloaders Logistics of multiple authors
Group Project	Motivation Potential to do more complicated tasks Potential to accomplish more as a group	Possibility of freeloaders Logistics and individual schedules

Student Reflection and Feedback

Cooperative learning strategies provide an opportunity for us to ask students to reflect on and assess their own contributions and those of their peers in group activities. This self-assessment is particularly valuable if done after a group project or exam since it encourages each student to consider the dynamics within the group and his contribution to the group task. This kind of self-reflection can have a positive impact on the individual's contribution to group activities, and consequently, on individual achievement and success in the course. Some instructors prefer also to use these informal assessment techniques instead of trying to grade group work during class.

Some instructors ask for daily or weekly feedback from the students in response to questions such as the following:

• What have you learned in this class?

• How (in what ways) have you contributed to the learning environment in the class today (or this week)?

• What were the main ideas, concepts, or techniques you learned today (or this week)? How well do you feel you understand them?

• What are some remaining issues or unclear aspects?

These questions might be given on a simple questionnaire that students fill out at the end of each class period or at the end of each week. The instructor might have the students write a two-minute paper or a journal entry responding to these or similar questions at regular intervals. Some respondents to our survey report that they mark these comments with a simple $(-, 0, +)$ rating system, while others use a numerical scale (say, 0 to 10 points). These strategies encourage students to be more reflective about learning as a process, and they provide an opportunity for continuing feedback between students and the course instructor.

Many instructors who use cooperative learning also report that asking for regular feedback from their students about what is working well and what is not working well is very helpful in making adjustments in their instruction throughout the semester. In processing their group functioning, students can be asked to jot down individual reflections and then to discuss their responses to questions such as the following:

• How well did we work together today as a group?

• What might we do differently next time?

At the time that a group project is being turned in, students can be asked to reflect on their individual contributions to the project. One instructor reported asking the students to write a sentence or two in response to each of the following questions on the day that a group project is turned in:

• What did you learn as you worked on this project?

• As your group worked on this project, what roles did each person in your group take on? (Was there a leader? . . . Did someone do library research? . . . Was someone primarily responsible for the writing? . . . What other roles did individuals take on as you worked on this project?)

• Did your group, or individuals within your group, collaborate with other groups? If so, how did your group collaborate with other groups? What were the benefits of this collaboration?

• What was your contribution to the group solution?

• If you had 500 points to distribute among the members of your group for each person's contribution to this project, how would you suggest these points be distributed? Why?

She has found that the responses of the students are usually quite candid and that students from the same group give generally consistent responses.

Some students are reluctant to report negatively about a classmate's performance. However, a question asking students how they would distribute 500 points among the members of their group can be posed in a way that invites students to affirm those who contributed more to the project. It can serve as a kind of litmus test of unbalanced participation among the group members.

This kind of reflection helps support the student in the typically unfamiliar environment of a cooperative classroom by offering opportunities for them to provide input to the instructor. It demonstrates for the students that the instructor is genuinely interested in improving the opportunities to learn the material of the course. These reflections might be written on student evaluation forms periodically throughout the course or in students' journals. Student management teams also can be used to obtain this kind of course feedback.

Class Participation

In a traditional classroom, class participation is sometimes used as a mechanism that allows an instructor to give the benefit of a subjective assessment, particularly to those students whose grades are borderline. In a classroom making use of cooperative learning strategies, it is possible to make the class participation component more explicit, even if still subjective. One way that this is typically done is to view the scores assigned to student feedback forms or journal entries as participation scores. This is one area where we find ourselves giving grades (admittedly highly subjective grades) in order to encourage students to take this work seriously.

Quizzes and Homework

Quizzes and daily homework also are essentially formative assessments. Some of us and some of the respondents to our survey report that homework is reviewed and not graded, but others report that they grade homework in order to motivate students to take it more seriously. Some instructors view quizzes as more summative than homework, but certainly less summative than a test.

Group Tests and Exams

In courses where cooperative learning is used in a significant way, tests may be given and marked in the same way as in courses that use more traditional instructional strategies. Alternatively, one or more of the tests may be a group test or may have a group component. Instructors who are using cooperative learning often try to find a balance between individual accountability and group accountability in assessing student achievement. The following question was included on our survey:

- If you used group testing, what percentage of the total test and examination grade was earned through group tests?

Responses	Number	Percent
10% or less	9	16. 1%
11–20%	13	23. 2%
21–30%	9	16. 1%
31–40%	6	10. 7%
41–50%	5	8. 9%
51–60%	0	0. 0%
61–70%	1	1. 8%
It varies	13	23. 2%
Total	56	100. 0%

Notice that more than half (55. 4%) of these respondents said that 30% or less of the total test and examination grade was earned through group tests, while fewer that 2% of these respondents said that more than 50% of the total test grade was based on group tests. Nearly sixty percent (58. 9%) of the respondents reported that between 11% and 50% of the total test and examination grade was earned through group tests. The issue of balance is particularly important in discussions about group exams. This requires careful consideration of the composition, administration, and grading of group exams. We say more about group exams in the next section.

Group Activities for Collaboration

Ideally, learning tasks are designed so that assessments are built into the activity itself. For example, when the student is asked to write a research paper, the written paper is evaluated as evidence that the student has learned something about the topic of this paper. The paper is used as evidence of what the student has learned. In a similar way, the product of a group activity should contain evidence that the individuals who participated in developing the product have learned something about the concepts embedded in the task. In developing tasks for cooperative learning, the idea is to structure the tasks in such a way that individual students have incentive for working together on the project, and everyone gets more from the activity by working together.

Since often the goal of the students is to maximize their individual grades, the requirements of the activity, including the requirement to collaborate with their group, must be designed to reward the kind of participation that is likely to increase individual learning. Somehow the graded requirements of the activity should reflect the learning that went on among the group members.

Why do we have students work together on course activities? Sometimes we do this for very practical or pragmatic reasons, such as sharing limited resources. Sometimes we ask students to discuss ideas or concepts because the effort to verbalize an idea helps them to clarify it in their own minds. Sometimes we ask students to work together because we see individual students accomplishing more as a part of a group than we could expect of them working as individuals.

Collaborating to Share Limited Resources

Perhaps the most common or natural way to foster a cooperative learning environment is to require students to share limited resources such as computers, other expensive technology, or copies of printed materials. Students in computer programming classes can often be observed in the computer lab engaged in conversations that are very productive for learning. Programming students often share ideas about how to think about difficult programming problems. These conversations among programming students led one of the authors to ask how she could design course assignments for mathematics classes that would invite students into the same kinds of productive dialog. She noted that students in a programming class are often required to turn in separate programs for individual assessments. They may be encouraged to discuss ideas with each other and required to give credits appropriately. If their conversations with each other lead to significant insights, they might be required to include documentary comments in the program listing. For example, "The insight to solve the problem in this way came from a conversation with . . ." is one such comment. If several students turn in similar program code with no attribution, all of them can be challenged to identify the code's source. These methods can be adapted to assignments for mathematics students.

Class activities can be designed so that students need to share limited copies of charts or text material. Sharing limited printed materials during a class session tends to get the students sitting closer together, asking questions about the material, and engaging each other in discussion. However, ubiquitous copier machines make it hard at times to require that students actually share these resources. One of the authors noted that on occasion, a student has slipped out of class and returned a few minutes later with sufficient copies for each group member. She sometimes simply asks the students to humor her

by working together from just the one copy during that class session.

Collaborating to Share Ideas about Important Concepts

A lecture can be punctuated at regular intervals by asking students to talk to each other for a few minutes about the ideas that have just been presented. An effective way to do this is to invite students to think quietly for a moment and write a response to a question in their notebooks, and then to share their responses with the students sitting next to them. This strategy gives all students an opportunity to begin to formulate an idea before talking with others.

After students have read a difficult passage, either in class or in the previous night's homework assignment, they can be directed to discuss particular challenging concepts in their groups. The more directed the focus questions, the more likely the students are to discuss the really difficult ideas.

If the students have been working on a lab activity, they can reflect together on the results, as they share observations and attempt to formulate conjectures that seem to be supported by their observations. These in-class discussions can be assessed informally by eavesdropping on the separate conversations. Or individuals from different groups can be asked to share with the whole class some of the ideas that were discussed in their groups. If the instructor calls on different students during different class periods, students come to expect that everyone must be able to articulate the ideas discussed in the group.

Collaborating on Group Projects

Many undergraduate courses include a major term project, which can provide an important opportunity for collaboration. However, if the group project is not well designed, the students can fall into the situation where the student who is perceived as the best student, i.e., the most likely to get the highest grade, does the greatest share of the work. Instead of group projects, each individual might be required to research and submit an individual paper. In this situation, several class periods toward the end of the semester might be reserved for individual reports on this research. The pitfall is that students learn to listen politely and encouragingly to each other without learning anything substantive from each other's reports. In both of these situations, the major term project is not really a significant opportunity for the whole class to learn something from the work done by their peers. So the question arises: Is there a way to structure this kind of major project assignment so that significant learning is likely? And, if so, how can these projects be assessed so that high grades are likely to be associated with significant actual learning?

One strategy is to assign a sequence of interrelated topics for individuals or groups to investigate and report to the class. If the topics depend on earlier presentations, individuals realize that they are responsible for understanding and building on the content of each other's presentations. This promotes both more active listening and greater accountability for the quality of each presentation.

One instructor reported that the departmental expectation (as reflected in the departmental syllabus) required that some topics from graph theory be included in the Discrete Mathematics course. Since the text she adopted for the course did not explicitly include these topics, she developed a sequence of five assignments, each of which required some library research. She assigned one of these to each of the five groups in the class. Each group was to study the assigned topic and make a presentation to the class. The first assignment, "What is a Graph? ," was a general introduction to the language of graph theory with several examples of problems that could be analyzed using simple graphs. The second assignment explored the strategy of coloring the vertices of the graph, and it included some problems where partitioning the vertices into different subsets would be helpful in investigating the problem. Another assignment investigated planar graphs, while a fourth assignment investigated circuits and paths in graphs. A fifth assignment investigated the use of graphs to determine whether a popular puzzle had a solution. The students responsible for each of these graph theory reports were encouraged to bring some problems for the class that illustrated the ideas they were reporting on. Topics from these presentations were included on the tests and final exam for the course. Since the material was not conveniently included in their textbooks (although the entire class did have the library references for each assignment), students realized that it was in their best interest to really understand the material as it was presented by each

group. As the students realized that they were being held responsible for material that was presented by the group reports, they listened much more attentively, and they asked each other questions based on their need to understand the material. Class discussions on "graph theory days," as the students called these class periods, were particularly lively.

Some classes have a naturally diverse student body. For example, in an upper-division course in Numerical Analysis for mathematics and computer science majors, some students may be stronger programmers and others may have a stronger mathematics background. A good group project would be to study pseudo-code of a mathematical algorithm and to write a computer program that correctly implements the algorithm. The computer science students might be responsible for the programming while the mathematics majors are responsible for developing appropriate data sets for the algorithm to test the program. After working together to develop the program and see that it runs correctly, each student is required to write a report on a specific aspect of the program or algorithm. Because the students have worked together to develop a common solution to the problem using the program, each student tends to have a deeper understanding of the algorithm, its requirements, and its limitations. Knowing that she will have to write an individual paper increases each student's level of concern about how well she understands the algorithm and its implementation. It seems reasonable to assign a group grade for the program and data sets as well as individual grades for the individual follow-up papers.

Developing good group problems is not easy. While it may be easier for an experienced instructor to develop an effective group problem than it is for a beginning instructor, even instructors experienced in working in a cooperative learning environment find that developing good problems for group investigation requires both time and creativity. The development and publication of textbooks and supplementary materials that support these strategies for mathematics courses at all levels would be helpful to instructors who are attempting to implement cooperative strategies into their classes.

One way to reinforce the importance of individual accountability for learning is to include a question or a problem on the next test similar to one that has been discussed and solved by the students working in groups. Those students who have worked hard on the group project usually find such test items relatively easy, while those who have not taken the group project seriously may have great difficulty in answering the questions on the test. These questions can help to raise each student's level of concern that he learn something from the group project. The students' answers give the instructor a measure of how much individual learning took place while the students were working together on the group project.

Collaborating During a Test

There are several ways to structure opportunities for student collaboration in testing situations. The authors have found the following strategies to be effective.

Following Test

A fairly simple testing strategy to implement (perhaps with a teaching assistant if the class is very large) is to allow a short group meeting during a test. The test format can be similar to a traditional in-class individual test, except that about two-thirds of the way through the test period, the students can meet in their groups for, say, ten minutes. During this meeting, they may discuss any of the test questions and the strategies they are using or attempting to use in answering the questions. But they may not write anything at all during the group meeting." All pencils and pens must be turned off!" This gives the students the benefit of checking some things with each other, but does not allow quite enough time for them to go over the entire test. They really have to make some choices about how to use the group-meeting time.

Group Test

One of three or four tests given during the course might be a group test. In this situation, the group is asked to turn in just one set of group responses to the test questions. The questions on the group test can be more challenging than students at their level of development might be expected to solve individually in the same time frame. A group test seems to work best if the groups are fairly well balanced with respect to ability. Students should be able to solve more sophisticated problems when working in a group than when working individually. Students working together can be expected to analyze open-ended questions and to develop a mathematical

idea beyond the presentation that has been given in the lecture or the assigned reading.

Before students are asked to work together on difficult problems in a test setting, they can be prepared for such a test by working together on in-class tasks requiring analysis of a complex situation or the construction of examples and counterexamples. If students can learn these skills and practice them under the pressure of an exam setting, they will be better prepared for the workplace.

Group testing raises an interesting question: Is it possible for a group to know more in some way than the individuals in the group, or does something happen when individuals collaborate that makes it possible for the group to perform in ways that exceed the possible performance of the individuals in the group? The authors do not offer an answer to this question here; it seems to be an interesting question for further research.

Composition and Administration of a Group Exam

The administration of a group test may occur either in class or out of class. Although we did not explicitly ask about time allowed for group tests on the survey, many of our survey respondents mentioned that students taking a test in groups needed more time than students working individually since they needed to discuss their problem-solving strategies and agree on their solutions. If a group test is to be administered in class, it may be appropriate to construct the test with fewer questions, which go into more depth, rather than more questions with relatively quick solutions. The instructor or a teaching assistant may proctor an out-of-class group test during an evening session, or the test may be a take-home test. Some instructors have expressed a preference for proctoring an out-of-class group exam because the take-home test may end up being similar to a group project. Some of the authors and respondents have allowed unlimited time for such a group exam and have found that students take several hours.

In order to help students focus on the mathematics and work to their fullest potential, instructors report that they strive to make the testing atmosphere as relaxed as possible. This can be done by finding a room where students have space to spread out their work, by creating a more congenial proctoring technique (for example, allowing students to trade hints for points), and even by allowing students to bring snacks and beverages or to order out for pizza.

The authors and some of the respondents to our survey have reported two essentially different approaches to having the students write solutions to the problems on a group test. One method is to allow the students to work together and write solutions collaboratively. The other approach is to allow students to discuss the problems orally while writing nothing down, after which each group member writes and submits solutions individually. Under either of these approaches, instructors have reported that the intention is to provide students with the opportunity of demonstrating personal ownership of the group's solutions. Individual write-ups can challenge freeloaders to confront their lack of participation in the group effort, and individually written solutions give the instructor an opportunity to assess how well each individual student understands the material. On the other hand, when the group has to develop and write up a single solution, they are forced to work harder to articulate their common solutions. This challenges individuals to work together toward a deeper understanding of the problems and their proposed solutions.

It does happen in the real world of our classrooms that some students may opt out of the challenging process of developing a true group solution to the problems that are posed. They may be content to rely on receiving the group grade while not making a serious contribution to the group's problem-solving effort. One way to dissuade such behavior is to follow a group test with an individual test based on the solutions of the problems that the group has worked on together.

Group Develops an Answer Key for the Test

A traditional in-class individual test with some challenging problems can be followed by an opportunity for the group to work together on the same questions before the next class period. The group turns in one set of group solutions for the entire test; essentially, the group is developing an answer key for the test they have just taken. The grade for this test can be a weighted average of the in-class individual work (promoting individual accountability) and the take-home group part. In this case, it is effective to make 10–20% of the test items sufficiently challenging that even the best students find it to their advantage to work with their group on

the test. Only those who have participated in the take-home part can receive credit for this portion. This testing strategy tends to encourage students to find and correct any errors that they made during the individual test. The weights for the two parts of the test might be adjusted by the instructor to reflect the difficulty of the test items.

Group Oral Exam Following an Individual Test

For a senior-level seminar class, a comprehensive exam with challenging problems and questions requiring research or experimentation can be given as a take-home exam. The students are on their honor to work individually on the exam for one or two weeks. On the day the exam is due, the students engage in a seminar discussion during which each member presents a solution and the group either accepts the solution as presented or the group comes to consensus about how to correct the solution. To encourage individual accountability, students are required to turn in individual work. Grades can be a weighted average of individual grades and the group grade on the oral presentations.

Grading of Group Assignments—Exams, Projects, and Lab Reports

Whenever students have to submit a single report or single write-up that expresses all their work, they have to work harder to understand what they are thinking individually. They also have to listen to each other to really understand what they are saying together. This gets at the core of the deepest benefits we see from observing students working together.

The grading of a group assignment is perhaps one of the most controversial issues in any discussion of cooperative learning in collegiate-level classes. At first glance it may seem that group grades give credit to some students for work done by their group members. While this is certainly a possibility, we would argue that credit can be given for group assignments in a reasonable and fair manner. If the solutions are written individually after the group discussion, each group member may receive an individual score based on her write-up. However, some instructors report giving each member a weighted average of her individual score and the group's average score. This weighted average is controversial since one student who performs poorly may pull down the group's average and thus pull down the score for each of his teammates. On the other hand, this grading scheme can motivate the group to work together in such a way that the stronger students help the weaker students to perform at a higher level. An additional advantage found when the disparity between the weaker students and the stronger students is not too great is that all the students reinforce their own understanding. They may also find errors through the process of explaining and justifying their own work to the others in the group.

When the group writes and submits a single solution paper for a test, the most commonly reported grading scheme is to award each individual in the group the same score. However, another scheme mentioned by our respondents is to take the group's test score, S, and multiply it by the number, n, of members in the group. When the assignment is returned to the group, the group members may decide how to share the nS points. If the group decides that everyone is equal, that's fine; if the group decides to award some members extra points for extra contributions, that's fine too. Certainly, the most common decision is for equal division of points among the group members, but this scheme does allow the group members an option for policing themselves.

There is a variety of strategies for assigning weights to group and individual work. Some alternatives and how they might affect group dynamics are described below.

• An assignment containing both a group and an individual component may be graded so that each group member receives a weighted average of the group score and her individual score. This method helps to identify freeloaders, especially when the individual component receives more weight than the group component.

For example, suppose that on a given test, each student receives a score that reflects one part group effort and two parts individual effort. It is reasonable to calculate the score for this test as a weighted average:

$$\frac{(\text{group score}) + 2 \cdot (\text{individual score})}{3}$$

Suppose that four students in a particular group receive individual scores of 96%, 85%, 82%, and 65%. This group's average score is 82% on this exam. Using this weighted average, the grades on this test for these individuals are

91%, 84%, 82%, and 73%. While the best student's grade in this group comes down from A to (perhaps) A−, the weakest student's grade may only have been raised from C− to C. This is enough to make it worth the effort it takes to work together effectively, while not actually giving away grades too easily.

• An individual exam or report may be graded individually. Then the average score of the group members is recorded as an additional grade for each member of the group. While this scheme is controversial, it provides a strong incentive for groups to work together toward a common goal.

• A group exam may be followed by an individual exam. This provides the instructor with an opportunity to assess the ability of the students to carry what they learned while working together into their own individual work. Again, this method can help to identify freeloaders. If the groups do not seem to be working together effectively (or at all), the instructor may offer bonus points based on a percentage increase in the group's average score on successive exams.

• The first test of the semester is given as a traditional individual test. Before the second test, the students are told that if everyone in the group either gets an A or shows improvement (of, say, five or more percentage points) on the second test, then everyone in the group will receive five extra credit points. This method tends to encourage some outside-of-class group study sessions in preparation for the test. In a tangible way, everyone in the group benefits if each individual improves or achieves at a high level.

• Following an individual exam, each group takes a copy of the exam home and reworks the problems together. They may use books, notes, computers or calculators, and other resources and essentially construct an answer key for themselves. If this group assignment is due at the next class session, it gives the students more immediate feedback on their individual performance and engages the students more deeply in an analysis of their own errors or misunderstandings.

Grades and Grading Schemes to Reflect Group Work

In any conversation about using cooperative learning groups in college or university classes, the question of grades soon arises. If significant portions of the class activities are done in groups, it seems reasonable to include group work in the assessment process. Yet it is often asked if it is fair to base individual grades on the work of the group. Is the product of the group work reflective of the achievements of the individuals in the group? Might the group task have been divided among the group members in such a way that each person in the group really understands or masters only a fraction of the whole? What should be done about freeloaders? Should students who do not participate or contribute to the group task share equally or at all in the group grade?

Research suggests that when cooperative learning is used, interpersonal sanctions are directed toward increasing individual achievement only if group rewards are based on some kind of sum of individual learning performance (Slavin, 1983b). In other words, the group needs to be rewarded for working effectively on the learning tasks. Assessment of effective group work must be based on some measure of individual achievement to avoid the situation where only the most able students do the work (Graves, 1991).

The question each of us grapples with is one of balance. Since we believe that group work contributes to individual learning achievement, how do we balance the various components that contribute to course grades so as to encourage greater individual learning performance? When determining the weights to be assigned to group and individual work, the instructor is actually making an implicit statement about her own philosophy concerning the purpose of the group work in the course. If the emphasis of the course is primarily on the mathematical content, the weights given to activities that contribute to the final course grade will tend to emphasize individual understanding of the content. On the other hand, if the instructor believes that it is important for students to develop and/or improve their skills in group processes, the weights will tend to give more emphasis to contribution or participation in the group processes.

The following question about how much of the student's course grade is earned through participation in group activities was included on our survey. Earlier in this chapter, a similar table showed what percentage of test and examination grades was based on group tests. This question about group activities in the course has a somewhat different focus.

- What percentage of a student's course grade is earned through group activities?

Responses	Number	Percent
10% or less	20	17. 1%
11–20%	37	31. 6%
21–30%	28	23. 9%
31–40%	12	10. 3%
41–50%	10	8. 5%
51–60%	3	2. 6%
61–70%	2	1. 7%
It varies	5	4. 3%
TOTAL	117	100%

Notice that nearly three-fourths (72. 6%) of the choices made by respondents were that 30% or less of the total course grade was earned through group activities, while only a small proportion of the respondents (4. 3%) reported basing more than half the total course grade on group activities.

Here are examples of three different grading schemes taken from course syllabi of some of the authors.

Example 1: Grading Scheme for a Second Semester Calculus Course

This is the second semester of a three-semester sequence of courses, which is usually taught by the same instructor. The instructor for this course knows most of the students in this class from the previous semester.

- Regular attendance, participation, homework, class and lab activities: 10%

Regular attendance is expected. Calculus has a well-deserved reputation for being difficult. If you miss a class, you are expected to find out what happened. Each class period you will be asked to fill out and turn in a class participation form. I will give you a score for participation and return the form to you in the next class.

Designing Assessment Activities

You are expected to attempt the activities, even if you don't get them all correct. Research in learning theory has shown that attempting the activities (whether or not you get the right answers) increases understanding and retention. We will spend some time in the lab each week. You will be expected to spend additional time with your group in the lab outside of class time.

There will be occasional (unannounced) quizzes. I do not give make-ups for quizzes. In general you will be able to work on the quizzes in your groups.

- Tests: 40–45%

There will be three tests. Some of the tests will have a part that you will be asked to do in your groups. The material to be covered on each test will be announced one or two class periods prior to the scheduled test date. Ordinarily, I do not give make-up tests; exceptions to this policy will be considered on a case-by-case basis.

- Benchmark (or Gateway) Tests: 10%

Benchmark testing is the department's way of assuring that students have achieved minimum levels of calculational competency. Although we will be using computers and calculators throughout this course, you will be expected to learn to do certain calculations by hand, and these will be indicated as we go along. There will be two equally-weighted benchmark tests: one near midterm, and the second one near the end of the course.

To pass each benchmark test on the first attempt, you must get nine or ten of ten problems completely correct; there will be no partial credit. If you pass on the first attempt, your score will be recorded as 100%.

If you do not pass a benchmark test on your first attempt, you may demonstrate that you have done some additional practice, and make an appointment with me to try the test once or twice again. To pass the benchmark test on a re-take, you must get nine or ten problems correct with no partial credits. If you eventually pass the test, your score will be recorded as the average of your first score and your passing score (which will be either 90% or 100%).

If you do not (eventually) pass a benchmark test, your score will be recorded as 0%.

- Project: 10%

There are many interesting problems that can be studied using the tools of calculus. There will be one project assignment that you will be encouraged to work on in your groups. This assignment will be available on February 23 and due on March 6.

- Final Exam: 25–30%

The cumulative final exam will contribute 25–30% to your overall grade for this course. Note that if you do better on the exam than your test average for the semester, the exam will carry more weight. On the other hand, if you are having a bad day on the day of the exam and your exam grade is lower than your test average, the average of your scores on the three tests will carry more weight.

In this example, the daily participation (attendance, participation, ungraded homework, class and lab activities) and project grades are group scores, while the benchmark tests and final exam are individual scores. Some portions of the three tests will include a group part, but the instructor has not committed herself to how much will be a group part. Individual students actually receive different daily participation scores. For example, a student receives no points for being absent. Everyone in the group receives the same grade on the project, but this contributes only 10% to the final course grade. So 20% of the grade is based on group work, and 35–40% of the grade is based on individual work. Some of the test grades, representing 40–45% of the course grade, will be based on group work, but the instructor has not specified the weights on this syllabus. She can make an adjustment depending on her observations of how well the groups are working together.

Example 2: Procedures and Grading Scheme for a Precalculus Course

This class meets four times per week, three times in the regular classroom (for lecture, discussion, and small- and large-group work) and once each week in the computer lab.

- You will need to have a scientific graphing calculator for this course. Texas Instruments TI-82 or TI-83 are recommended. The TI-82 will be demonstrated in class.

- Homework assignments will be given daily. These assignments are due the next class period after they are assigned.

- Plan to spend 8 to 10 hours per week in study and doing assignments for this course outside of class.

- There will be twelve computer labs, eight short quizzes, three 1-hour tests, and a comprehensive 2-hour final exam.

- Requests for alternate test times will only be considered if they are made in advance and are necessitated by some emergency.

- Some activities, including all computer labs, will be organized as group investigations.

- Course grades will be based on the labs (300 points), quizzes (200 points), tests (300 points), and final exam (200 points).

In this scheme, each lab report is a group effort and is worth 25 points, 5 points for attendance and 20 points for quality of the report. Individuals in each group share the same score except for adjustments made for absence or nonparticipation. The lab reports represent 30% of the total course grade. The other 70% are essentially individual scores, but this depends on the possible use of group testing and the weights given to that on specific tests.

Example 3: Grading Scheme for a General Education Course in Mathematical Models

Course grades will be based on the following number of possible points:

Attendance	100
Journal	100
Group Projects/Presentations	200
Three tests	300
Final exam	100
TOTAL	800

In this scheme, 25% (200 points) of the course grade is directly related to group effort. However, the attendance component is also a group participation score and the journal connects with group work in many ways. The weight given to testing in this course is lower than that given in other courses taught by the same instructor.

Conclusion

Assessment is an overloaded term used in different contexts for different purposes, thus blurring its meaning for all of them. While the problems of assessing the work of our students are not unique to cooperative learning, cooperative learning creates new opportunities and new challenges.

In the context of a particular course, assessment of student learning is usually linked with grading and is an important issue. The final course grade that a student receives often determines whether or not a student can take the next course, or which of several possible courses a student might take next. Therefore, instructors are rightly concerned that the final course grade be an honest assessment of the student's knowledge and ability. However, assessment is also used to motivate the student, to apprise the instructor and the student of the student's progress in learning the course material, and in some cases, to evaluate teaching effectiveness.

When we ask our students to work in groups in the classroom and laboratory, and when we ask them to get together to do their homework, how do we test them on the course content? While using cooperative learning in our classrooms, the authors of this volume and many of our colleagues have found that all the traditional forms of testing can still be used and that additional modes of assessment become available. Individual progress can be observed and assessed through class participation, individually-written journal entries, group projects and homework, and group quizzes and exams. In this chapter we have discussed some of the ways that we have used to test, assess, and assign grades to our students. We have reflected on what seemed to work for us and why we think it worked.

The process of assessment and grading is complicated and highly personal. Each instructor needs to make decisions that reflect his own philosophies of mathematics and mathematics learning as well as the philosophies of colleagues in the department or the institution. The discussion and examples given above attest to a wide variety of possible approaches to this topic. Reflecting on one's own assessment practices helps to reveal an underlying personal philosophy of assessment. As this becomes clear, new questions can be asked that help each instructor make positive changes in her practice.

Designing Assessment Activities

      Reliability, validity, and fairness are issues in assessment, whether in a cooperative learning environment or not. These issues need to be addressed in relation to the examples given above and will continue to drive a continuing discussion and research into these and other appropriate methods and techniques of assessment.

Chapter 5

Learning Theory and Constructing Cooperative Learning Activities

Anne Brown, David J. DeVries, Ed Dubinsky, Georgia Tolias

Introduction

As cooperative learning gains in popularity, a great many examples of activities are becoming available for teachers to adapt for use in their classrooms. In deciding whether to use an existing activity, or in thinking about designing a new one, we might first ask whether the activity is appropriate for our students, whether it will hold their attention and, most importantly, whether it will help make significant improvements in their learning. The dismal state of mathematics education today and the needs of our society for the immediate future, as well as for the long run, require major improvements in learning. It seems clear that we are not going to achieve this by continuing to teach in the way we always have, nor by making only minor adjustments in what we do and how we think about the learning and teaching enterprise. Asking deeper questions about how we choose and design activities can help us begin to see how to make these changes.

Making changes in one's teaching practice is a difficult process to carry out with any consistency; it is very hard to avoid doing what we have always done, what worked for us as students and what feels most natural in a teaching situation. Many teachers make choices about their approach to teaching a particular subject without being sure that they will have more than a modicum of the desired effect on student learning. Indeed, it can be argued that one

reason that many of our students do not learn very much mathematics is that too few of us are willing or able to make major changes in what we do in our teaching.

It is certainly the case that most mathematics teachers are thoughtful about their teaching. Readers of this book are, no doubt, especially concerned about their own teaching practice and are seeking ways to improve the results of instruction. But even the best intentions may not be enough to overcome the difficulties inherent in changing teaching practice. A central difficulty is that the choices teachers make about what to do and what not to do in their classes are also influenced, often unconsciously, by beliefs both about how students learn and about the nature of the mathematical content that is to be learned (Thompson, 1992). We assert that ignoring the effect of one's beliefs leads inevitably to continuing to do what one has always done.

In this chapter, we offer a suggestion that provides both an explanation for the lack of major change in learning and teaching as well as a possible means of achieving such change. We believe that when teachers think about what they will be doing in the classroom, they seldom consciously incorporate a theoretical perspective about the nature of the mathematics to be learned and how a student is going to learn it. For example, often a teacher will try to improve learning by including group activities without considering whether changes in how the students are expected to actually learn the mathematics are needed. Such changes in practice will likely have only a slight impact on student learning because the design of the new activities still reflects the teacher's previous, possibly unconscious, beliefs about mathematics and learning.

As an alternative approach to effecting change in teaching practice, we propose that teachers consciously choose a theory of the nature of the mathematics that is to be learned, together with a theory of how that learning can take place, and then explicitly derive their teaching practice from those theories. This approach is based on the assumption that a theoretical perspective can affect one's teaching practice through relating it, in the context of making teaching choices, to one's beliefs about the following two fundamental questions:

1. What is the nature of the mathematical content to be learned?

2. How can students learn this content?

Making lasting change in teaching practice is more feasible when it is clearly related to the teacher's current practice and the teacher is fully aware of just what is changing and what is not. Thus, it is essential that the teacher examine his views about these questions, how those views relate to the teacher's normal teaching practice, and what changes adopting a particular theory will require. In selecting a theory to adopt, a teacher should be aware of the ways in which this theory resonates with his present beliefs and practices, and the ways in which it does not.

It follows from all this that it would make sense in developing cooperative learning activities to begin with a theoretical perspective on how people learn mathematics (an epistemology) and coordinate it with classroom practice (a pedagogy). We would argue that the issue is never one of balancing two competing concerns but rather one of synthesizing epistemology and pedagogy.

Once an activity has been implemented in a classroom, there is a temptation to conclude that it was successful if the students enjoyed it and it held their attention. This is no small accomplishment in today's world. But justifying a claim of success requires more detailed analysis and information: what was the nature of the mathematics that was to be learned, and how did that learning happen, or not happen?

The two types of theoretical perspectives considered here (epistemological and pedagogical) are not independent. We submit that theories about how students learn mathematics are determined, at least in part, by theories concerning the nature of the mathematics to be learned.

The following are four general categories of theories which we feel cover most of the ideas that have been put forward about the nature of an area of mathematical content. Each is presented with a statement of how someone adopting that type of theory might view his role as a mathematics educator in helping students to learn that content, and a theoretical hypothesis about how students learn which is consistent with that role. See also (Dubinsky, 1994).

- **View 1:** One might believe that an area of mathematics to be learned is a body of knowledge that has been discovered by our society, over several hundred years, and that we must pass it on to future generations by transferring the knowledge to the minds of our students. As a result, a teacher might see his role as one who presents the mathematics as clearly as possible to students. This is consistent with the theoretical hypothesis that students learn spontaneously. That is, students learn mathematics individually and through exposition, by looking at printed material or listening to a speaker. According to this theoretical position, little can be done directly, beyond making clear presentations, to help them learn. To encourage students to acquire knowledge spontaneously, one would present the material to students clearly, in verbal, written, or pictorial form, and expect them to learn it on their own.

- **View 2:** One might believe the mathematics to be learned is a set of canonical structures, techniques, and algorithms for solving standard problems. If this describes one's conception of the nature of mathematics, then one might present, or help the student develop, working definitions of these structures and processes, and then ask students to apply them in a wide variety of standard problem situations. This is consistent with the theoretical hypothesis that students learn mathematics inductively. That is, students learn mathematics by working with many examples, extracting common features and important ideas from these experiences, and organizing that information in their minds. Someone who holds the position that students learn inductively in acquiring concepts and relationships would design activities that give students extensive experience working with examples that are sequenced in such a way that students induce the concepts and relations from those experiences.

• **View 3:** One's theoretical hypothesis might be that the essence of an area of mathematics is in its power to describe, explain, and predict phenomena. One's teaching might then involve the examination of topics in the physical or social sciences with an emphasis on the role of mathematics. This is consistent with the position that students learn mathematics pragmatically, in the context of problems in other fields. To encourage students to learn mathematics through applications, the teacher would present students with many situations from the physical and social sciences that require application of the mathematical content of interest.

• **View 4:** One might make the theoretical hypothesis that the mathematics to be learned is a set of ideas that individual and collective thought has created. One's teaching techniques might then be to try to help students construct these ideas for themselves. This is consistent with the position that students learn mathematics constructively. That is, students learn mathematics by making mental constructions to deal with mathematical situations. To encourage students to construct mathematical thought, the teacher would precede the design of instruction with a study of what mental constructions might be involved in learning a particular area of mathematics, of how those constructions might be made, and of what can be done to encourage students to make them. Then, she would design instruction based on the findings.

How might teacher beliefs affect the design and use of cooperative learning activities? Here are some possibilities. One who believes mathematics is transmitted and absorbed is likely to rely heavily on lecture as the primary classroom activity. Cooperative learning would be used mainly to reinforce what has been communicated. Instructors who believe that students learn inductively would design activities that can be done individually or in groups, where the purpose of using groups is to provide support or to provide a mechanism for generating and analyzing multiple examples. For one who believes that students learn mathematics through

the use of applications, cooperative learning would tend to be centered on group projects that investigate physical or social phenomena. For one who believes students learn constructively, the use of group learning would be considered essential because of the value of social interaction in fostering mental constructions and in the examination of alternative student understandings. In the next section, we will illustrate these four possibilities in more detail.

The Effect of Beliefs on the Design of Activities

In this section, we explore how a teacher's views on the nature of mathematics and mathematics learning might affect his design of cooperative learning activities. Choosing a specific mathematical topic, we imagine ourselves as teachers who hold each of the four theoretical positions in turn, and describe a cooperative learning activity that we could design to help students learn it. Since the individual who designs a learning activity may unconsciously hold more than one belief about mathematics and learning, the influence of a variety of beliefs might be detectable in any activity.

We assume that each activity is presented in a class where the students have studied the basics of modular addition and multiplication. The goal of each activity is the same: to engage the students in learning about multiplicative inverses $\bmod m$ and to use this knowledge to solve equations of the form $ax = b \bmod m$. Also of interest is the use of that knowledge in the context of a problem from cryptography; a focus on congruences $\bmod 26$ results from the identification of the alphabet with the set $\{1, 2, \ldots, 26\}$. Our choice of coding as a topic was inspired by an example that appeared in *The Mathematics Teacher* (Volume 89, Number 9, page 757, Dec. 1996).

Activity 1

If the teacher believes that mathematics is a body of knowledge to be communicated, and that students learn spontaneously, then she might transmit this knowledge using a lecture format. This could be followed by exercises which students can do in groups as a means of reinforcing the content of the lecture.

An essential component here is the teacher's preparation of a well-organized and logically arranged lecture on how to solve linear congruence equations. The teacher might begin by reminding students that solving linear equations of the form $ax = b$ over the real numbers requires multiplication by the inverse of a and the associative property. These ideas could be illustrated by solving some specific linear equations. Then the teacher might explicitly relate this to the goal of finding analogous methods for solving linear congruences by defining multiplicative inverses mod m, and showing how to use this to solve equations of the form $ax = b \bmod m$. To illustrate that not all elements have multiplicative inverses mod m, the teacher might construct a multiplication table mod 5 and one for mod 6. The teacher might use these tables to solve the equation $3x = 4 \bmod 5$ and to show that $3x = 5 \bmod 6$ has no solution. Finally, the teacher could end the lecture by showing how this knowledge can be applied to solve problems in cryptography. Specifically, the teacher could present the context of encoding and decoding messages as problems involving equations of the form $c = ap \bmod 26$, where p is the plaintext letter and c is the ciphertext letter. The teacher could point out that decoding a message requires solving the equation for p given values for c and a. The teacher concludes the lecture and directs students to work in groups on the following activity:

1. Construct a multiplication table mod 9.

2. Find the multiplicative inverse (if one exists) for each of 1, 2, 3, 4, 5, 6, 7, and 8.

3. Use what you have found in problem 2 to solve the following congruences:

$$4x = 7 \bmod 9 \quad 5x = 4 \bmod 9 \quad 7x = 8 \bmod 9$$

4. Construct the rows of the mod 26 multiplication table corresponding to the numbers 6, 9, 11, and 13.

5. Which of the numbers listed in problem 4 has an inverse?

6. Use the inverse of $9 \bmod 26$ to decode DGAUQ, which was encoded using $9p = c \bmod 26$.

7. Break your group into pairs. Encode a short message for your partner using $11p = c \bmod 26$. Trade messages and decode your partner's message.

In this activity, the general approach is to lay out as clearly as possible the mathematical ideas and to illustrate them with examples in a lecture/discussion format. The primary purpose of the group activity is reinforcement: rather than go beyond the lecture, the students apply the ideas in the same way as was done in the lecture. Student discussion might center on identifying which aspects of the lecture apply in each situation. Group work is not essential but may make the exercises more enjoyable than they would be otherwise.

Activity 2

If the teacher believes that mathematics is a set of canonical structures and generalized techniques, and that students learn inductively, then he would provide students with a setting in which they can solve many related problems, formulate generalizations by noting common aspects among the problems, and apply their understandings to a wider set of problem situations. Specifically, the teacher might begin with a brief summary of that day's mathematical focus as a means of setting the stage and then direct students to work in groups on the activity described below.

First, the students might be introduced to the idea that addition can be used to define a transformation on the set $[0, 1, 2, \ldots, m-1]$ through working particular examples such as problem 1 below. The student also sees the role of additive inverses in reversing these transformations.

1. Make a table for addition mod 7. We use the tuple notation $X = [0, 1, 2, 3, 4, 5, 6]$ to denote the top row of the table.

   a) Use tuple notation to write the row Y that you get by adding 3 to each entry of X. We can denote this transformation as $y = (x + 3) \bmod 7$.

   b) Use tuple notation to write the row Z that you get by adding 5 to each entry of X. Write this in an equation that is similar in form to the equation in part a.

   c) How could you reverse the transformation of part a? That is, what would you have to add to each entry Y to obtain X? This number is called the *additive inverse* of 3 mod 7. What happens when you add this number to both sides of the equation in part a?

d) Find the additive inverse of 5 mod 7. What happens when you add this number to both sides of the equation in part b?

In the next two exercises, the student sees that transformations of the set $\{0, 1, \ldots, m-1\}$ could also be based on multiplication. The intent is to highlight the similarities and differences among the various transformations, including how they are expressed as equations, how the concept of inverse is involved, and whether or not the transformations can be reversed.

2. Make a multiplication table mod 7. Again, let $X = [0, 1, 2, 3, 4, 5, 6]$ denote the top row of the table.

a) Write the row Y obtained by multiplying each entry of X by 3. In an equation, we would denote this transformation by $y = 3x \bmod 7$.

b) Write the row Z obtained by multiplying each entry of X by 6. Write an equation that describes this transformation.

c) How could you reverse the transformation of part a? That is, what would you have to multiply by each entry of Y to obtain X? This number is called the *multiplicative inverse* of 3 mod 7. What happens when you multiply both sides of the equation in part a by this number?

d) Find the multiplicative inverse of 6 mod 7. Multiply each entry of Z by this number to illustrate how to reverse the multiplication of the entries of X by 6. Observe what happens when you multiply both sides of the equation in part b by this number.

e) What number must the row $[0, 5, 3, 1, 6, 4, 2]$ be multiplied by to obtain X? How can you solve the equation $w = 5x \bmod 7$ for x?

3. Consider multiplication mod 8, so the top row of the table would be $X = [0, 1, 2, 3, 4, 5, 6, 7]$.

a) Multiply each entry of X by 3 to obtain the row Y.

b) Reverse the transformation of part a, that is, find a number that you can multiply by each entry of Y to obtain X.

c) Multiply each entry of X by 6 to obtain

the row Z.

d) Can you find a number that you can multiply by each entry of Z to obtain X? Explain.

This work with small moduli is expected to adequately prepare the student for the subsequent exercises, which are intended to help the student to induce the features of transformations based on multiplication and then apply this knowledge to cryptography.

4. Consider multiplication mod 26. Make a conjecture as to whether multiplication by each of 6, 9, 11, and 13 can be reversed. Test your conjecture by finding the rows of the multiplication table mod 26 that correspond to each of these factors. Find the reverse transformation for each number that has a multiplicative inverse mod 26.

5. The mathematical ideas in exercise 4 can be applied in the context of cryptography to encode and decode messages. Assign the letters A through Z the numbers 1 through 26 and use your results from exercise 4 to encode the message, THIS MESSAGE IS SECRET, with the following transformation: $3p = c \bmod 26$. Here, p is the number corresponding to the plaintext letter and c is the number corresponding to the ciphertext letter. What transformation would you use to decode a message that was encoded with this transformation?

6. Break your group into pairs. Encode a short message for your partner using $11p = c \bmod 26$. Trade messages and decode your partner's message.

7. Which elements in $\{0, 1, 2, \ldots, 25\}$ could play the role of an encoding multiplier? Explain.

Here, the teacher's intention is that the students work cooperatively to explore the mathematical content through a sequence of exercises that lay the groundwork for the necessary generalizations. Because the teacher does not explain the content prior to the beginning of the activity, the opportunity to generate and exchange ideas with a group of peers could be critical to a student's learning of the mathematics.

Activity 3

If the teacher believes that the nature of mathematics lies in its use as a practical tool to solve problems from other fields, and that students learn pragmatically in the context of applications, then she might begin by describing the features of the situation and determining which mathematical tools relate to the particular mathematical model. The teacher might introduce the general problem of encoding and decoding messages and provide an appropriate historical backdrop for the group activity.

As a result, the teacher might discuss the encryption method used by Julius Caesar—named the Caesar cipher—in which each letter of the alphabet shifts a given number of letters to the right to produce the encrypted letter. The teacher would explain how to model the encoding process using an equation of the form $c = (p + n) \bmod 26$ and how solving this equation for p provides a mechanism for decoding messages.

Reflecting on the features of the mathematical model for the Caesar cipher, the teacher might point out the importance of scrambling the numbers 1 through 26 by some rule that can be undone. The teacher could ask students to suggest other types of rules, or simply point out that students will see other possible encoding processes in the exercises. Now that a context has been established and a mathematical model, which describes it, has been illustrated, the teacher can direct the students to work in groups on the following activity:

1. Encode the following message using the Caesar cipher, $c = (p + 3) \bmod 26$: THIS IS A SECRET MESSAGE

2. Given that the following message was encoded using the above Caesar cipher, decode it to get back the original message: WKLVL VKRZZ HGHFL SKHU

3. Suppose you now decide to encode the word FREEDOM using the following formula $11p = c \bmod 26$. Set up a correspondence table between the letters of the word and the corresponding ciphertext letters as in the example below:

Plaintext letter	L	I	N	E	A	R
Plaintext number	12	9	14	5	1	18
Ciphertext number	2	21	24	3	11	16
Ciphertext letter	B	U	X	C	K	P

4. Break your group into pairs and encode a short message using the above cipher equation. Exchange encoded messages with the other pair and try to decode each other's message.

5. To systematically decode a message that was encoded with $11p = c \bmod 26$, you could use an equation of the form $p = dc \bmod 26$ to find the plaintext letter when given the ciphertext letter. Note that d is the value of p when $c = 1$, so you can find the value of d by finding the plaintext number that corresponds to the ciphertext number one. The number d is called the *multiplicative inverse* of $11 \bmod 26$. Use this value of d to decode the word CEWKBA that has been encoded with the equation $11p = c \bmod 26$.

6. Suppose you decide to use the equation $c = 12p \bmod 26$ to encode a message. Would you be able to decode messages encoded by this equation? Explain.

In this activity, it is the application that is the primary focus and the mathematical ideas emerge as a result of working with the application. Many instructors believe that using an application of mathematics as a point of entry facilitates student discussion of the mathematical content. As in the inductive activity, the group work provides support and an opportunity to exchange and develop their ideas about the mathematics and its role in modeling problems in a particular context.

Activity 4

If the teacher believes that mathematics is a set of ideas that the student must construct in his mind, then the teacher approaches the design of an activity on this topic by first identifying the type of mental constructions that might support an understanding of a method of solving linear congruences mod m. This analysis will lead to the design of activities intended to foster the development of those constructions in the minds of the students, as well as constructions that relate to applying that knowledge to cryptography.

In the following activity, more so than in the others in this section, the influence of a specific learning theory will be seen. We assert that the design of instruction can be informed by the view that learning mathematics consists in making mental constructions only if the teacher makes a conscious theoretical decision about the nature of the constructions and how they might be made. Designing activities without making such a decision would suggest that the teacher believes that the constructions will occur spontaneously or perhaps are a matter of induction, in which case one of the other views predominates. For many topics, this decision can be based on research into the learning of mathematical concepts.

The design of this activity is derived from a particular constructivist theory of mathematical knowledge: action-process-object-schema (APOS) theory, which has been used by many researchers with some success. The interested reader can consult Asiala et al. (1996), and Dubinsky and McDonald (1996) for more details about this theory. While the theory guides the design of the instruction, only further observations and assessments can gauge the success of the instruction in improving student learning. The goal of the activity is to foster mental constructions related to solving the linear congruence $ax = b \bmod m$. Emphasizing the perspective that multiplication by $a \bmod m$ is a process that acts on the set $\{0, 1, \dots, m-1\}$, the activity is intended to guide the student in making mental constructions that relate to the properties of this process, to reversing the process, and to realizing that the process of multiplication by $a^{-1} \bmod m$ has the same effect as the reversed process.

Prior to this class session, the students would have completed exercises like 1 and 2 below. These exercises are intended to provide an experiential base for the action of multiplication by $a \bmod m$. As the learner reflects on them, he begins to internalize the actions as a mental process. Once this is accomplished, the learner can imagine running through, can reason about, and can reverse the steps of this multiplication process without having to actually carry it out.

1. For the entries in this table, $c = 3p \bmod 8$. Fill in the missing entries. Repeat the exercise with $c = 6p \bmod 8$. Compare the tables and make a note of any similarities or differences you observe.

p	1	2	3	4	5	6	7	0
c								

2. For the entries in this table, $c = 3p \bmod 26$. Fill in the missing entries. Repeat the exercise with $8p \bmod 26$. Compare the tables and make a note of any similarities or differences you observe.

p	4	6	9	10	13	17	23
c							

The class session would begin with the group members discussing their results and observations from the previous exercises. The groups will continue with exercises 3 and 4, which are intended to focus attention on the role of the multiplier (rather than on the entries of the table, or the inputs and outputs of the process). The idea here is to encourage thinking about the process separately from the objects it acts upon, so that the process of multiplication by $a \bmod m$ becomes an object of thought for the student.

3. The table below was created by multiplication by $a \bmod 9$, that is, the corresponding equation is $c = ap \bmod 9$. Find the value of a. Describe in words what you did to find the value of a. Fill in the remaining entries.

p	2	6	4	8	1	3	5	7	0
c	5	6	1	2					

4. Form two pairs in your group. Each pair is to invent a "find the missing multiplier" exercise like problem 3 for the other pair, using multiplication mod 13 instead of mod 9. Trade exercises and solve them. Discuss your solutions as a group.

Exercises like the next three are intended to lead students to construct the reversal of the process of multiplication by $a \bmod m$, to relate it to the process of multiplication by $a^{-1} \bmod m$, and to examine its role in the solution of linear congruences $\bmod m$. It is expected that, as students think about the idea that the process of multiplication by $a^{-1} \bmod m$ has the same effect as the reversal of multiplication by a, they will begin to think about them as being the same object, and refer to them by the same name.

5. Find the missing entries if $c = 5p \bmod 26$. Describe in words how you found each entry.

p	1		4		13	
c		1		4		6

6. Reading from the table in the preceding problem, find the element b that, when multiplied by 5, yields $1 \bmod 26$. This number is called the multiplicative inverse of $5 \bmod 26$. What happens when you multiply both sides of the equation $c = 5p \bmod 26$ by b?

7. Solve the equation $11p = c \bmod 26$ for p in terms of c. Use the transformed equation to fill in the missing entries in the table below, and check that the entries satisfy $11p = c \bmod 26$.

p						
c	9	11	18	4	1	23

At this point, the instructor might conduct a discussion that tries to get the students to focus on the mental constructions it was hoped they made in the course of working on the exercises. Such discussions can be particularly effective (and work with large classes) if the instructor is able to conduct them as a discussion among groups, rather than among individuals. The idea is to get each group discussing a point among themselves and then present the group's view to the entire class.

Finally, students work exercises that implement the entire encryption and decryption algorithms. Seeing multiplication by $a \bmod m$ and multiplication by $a^{-1} \bmod m$ as reverse processes is hypothesized to support an understanding of the dynamics of the encoding/decoding process.

8. Translate the literal plaintext below to numerical plaintext p and encode it using $c = 11p \bmod 26$. Translate the numerical ciphertext c to literal ciphertext.

	L	I	N	E	A	R
p						
c						

9. The word shown below was obtained through encryption by multiplication by $3 \bmod 26$. Decipher the word.

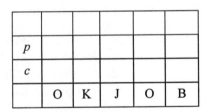

p						
c						
		O	K	J	O	B

From a constructivist point of view, the students' discussion of the exercises in their groups is an essential part of the activity. That is, it is recognized that just working through the exercises might not be sufficient to foster the growth of the necessary mental constructions. Reflections on the exercises and comparisons of alternative student understandings are theorized to play critical roles in the construction of new mathematical knowledge. It is worth noting that there is also a role for lecture in this approach. Since the activities occur prior to any whole-class discussion of the mathematics, the teacher might give an interactive lecture following the group activity with the aim of summarizing the mathematics that the students were expected to have learned.

While we have presented the four activities in this section as ones that follow from particular beliefs about mathematics and learning, it should be noted that some activities could be used to support a variety of beliefs and teaching approaches. That is, the essence of the belief is contained not in the activity directly, but in how the teacher uses that activity.

Also, even if our views on how students learn directly affect the design of our activities, the responses of our students may not fit our expectations. Often students will interpret or revise the demands of the activity to fit what they see as their own needs for learning. For example, when students are faced with an activity in which they are expected to learn constructively or pragmatically, they might well respond by asking the teacher for template examples. The point is that even if teachers design activities consistent with their own views on mathematics and on learning, the beliefs and the consequent responses of the students will also affect what occurs.

Our aim in this section was both to motivate the reader to examine her own views on mathematics and mathematics learning, and to illustrate how changing one's views might result in a change in practice. In the next section, we present one further example of how instruction can be based on a learning theory. In this case, the approach illustrated is one that has been tested through formal research.

A Role for Research in the Development of Cooperative Learning Activities

We asserted in the first section that it is very difficult to change one's teaching practice. We have also pointed out that one way to bring about change in teaching practice is by developing activities that are explicitly based on one's beliefs about mathematics and mathematics learning. In the second section, we gave four examples of how that might be done, with activity 4 being the most explicit example of a conscious application of a particular theory. The present form of activity 4 should be viewed as a first approximation of what a teacher who has chosen a constructivist theory of learning might do. The teacher has available two types of assessment of the effectiveness of the activity:

examining whether the hypothesized mental constructions appeared to be made by the students, and evaluating whether the mathematical performance of the students was as expected. The teacher would consider the results of those assessments in making adjustments to his description of the required mental constructions and the design of instruction for this topic in the future. The role of research in this process is the topic of this section.

Our final example will illustrate how making a decision to base instruction on a learning theory can lead to improved learning. The example concerns the learning of mathematical induction, which is known to be a perplexing topic for many undergraduates. Research literature on this subject (Dubinsky, 1986 and Dubinsky, 1989b) suggests that one of the difficulties students have with proof by induction is at the very beginning. The problem of showing that a certain proposition involving an arbitrary integer is true for all (sufficiently large) values of the integer is apparently new and quite difficult for most students. From a constructivist viewpoint, we would say that understanding this problem requires constructing a (mental) function which accepts a positive integer n, formulates a proposition in terms of n, and returns a value of true or false for each value of n.

Through research that included interviewing students about their understanding of induction, it was found that modeling this problem as a function in a mathematical programming language such as ISETL helps students see how to begin. The instruction on induction therefore includes activities that provide a base of experience with writing such functions. For example, students are asked to determine whether a gambling casino with only $300 and $500 chips can pay out any amount of money, beyond a certain minimum, within the nearest $100. Students begin their investigation of this problem by writing a computer program that accepts a positive integer and returns a Boolean value, *i.e.,* either true or false. They typically come up with a solution like the following.

```
P:=func (n)
if is _integer(n) and n > 0 then
return (exists x, y in [0. . n
div 3] | 3*x + 5*y = n)
end;
end;
```

Running this program for the first nine values of *n* gives the output shown in the second line below.

```
P(1);  P(2);  P(3);  P(4);  P(5);
P(6); P(7); P(8); P(9);
false; false; true; false; true;
true; false; true; true;
```

The process of writing this program apparently helps the student see that what is being returned is the value of an expression, and that some expressions have values that are numbers and others, like this one, have Boolean values. As a result, the student should now be able to think about a function that returns a truth-value for each positive integer. Put another way, the student has made a certain kind of mental construction related to understanding mathematical induction.

This activity exemplifies a successful approach to teaching mathematical induction that was developed through a research-based cycle of design, implementation, and assessment (Dubinsky, 1989b). The approach is markedly different from the traditional methods of teaching this topic and is certainly not one a teacher might come up with by making only minor adjustments in her teaching practice. Successes like this provide evidence that major changes in how undergraduate mathematics is taught and learned can be achieved when teachers are willing to choose a specific theory of learning and base the design and revision of their teaching practice on that theory. To reiterate: instead of relying on what seems most natural to oneself (which we argue usually maintains the status quo), the teacher chooses to rely on the tenets of a theory of learning to inform the design of instruction. After observing the results of instruction, the teacher can better assess whether applying the theory leads to improvements in student learning. If necessary, the instruction, the theory, or both may be revised as a result of the assessment.

We have described in this chapter how a significant change in one's outlook on teaching can result in real improvement in student learning. We now challenge the reader to go beyond examining his own beliefs about mathematics and learning, and to consider adopting a learning theory that is being developed through research. There is a small but growing body of research on the teaching and learning of undergraduate mathematics that the reader can consult to see what particular theories of mathematical learning are being developed and what

they could mean to a teacher's practice. The reader might find publications such as Dubinsky, Kaput, and Schoenfeld (1994, 1995, 1998), Harel and Dubinsky (1992), and Kaput and Dubinsky (1994) helpful in beginning this challenging process of change.

Chapter 6

Approaches to Cooperative Learning from Various Perspectives

Elizabeth C. Rogers, Neil A. Davidson, Barbara E. Reynolds,
Bronislaw Czarnocha, Martha B. Aliaga

Introduction

When a student learns a new mathematical idea, does he discover it? When a student proves a theorem, is she constructing something new or is she discovering something that exists but that she has not seen before? As teachers of mathematics, we make numerous decisions about what we will teach and how we will teach it based on our understanding of how we ourselves have learned mathematics and how we think others learn mathematics. Taken together, these decisions about content and pedagogical approach reflect our beliefs about the nature of mathematics and how people acquire mathematical knowledge.

One theory of learning is based on a belief that an individual learner makes a progression from Actions, to Process, to Objects, to Schema. Curriculum based on this theory typically consists of activities that students attempt before a concept is presented formally. Class discussion then leads students to reflect on what they observed while doing the activities, and follow-up exercises allow students to practice and solidify their newly acquired knowledge. This cycle of Activities, Class discussion, and Exercises is credited to Ed Dubinsky and is known as the ACE-cycle. The activities include open-ended questions and guided

explorations, and they frequently ask the students, who are working together in cooperative groups, to make conjectures relating to the development of the concepts. Class discussion may include brief lectures in which the instructor draws together ideas that the students have expressed. After students have made some observations about what they were thinking as they attempted the activities, the instructor may offer explanations or state mathematical principles that are just at the edge of the students' mathematical knowledge. Exercises that follow the class discussion include a full range of typical mathematics homework problems, including routine computations, word problems of varying levels of complexity, proofs of the underlying mathematical concepts, and problems requiring students to extend ideas that were discussed in class.

Another theoretical perspective is that of guided discovery or discovery learning. In the late 1960's, Lee Shulman (1968, 1970) wrote a classic paper comparing two theories of learning and teaching: the open-ended, exploratory discovery/inquiry approach of Jerome Bruner (1960, 1966) and the highly prescriptive, goal-directed, behavioral-learning-hierarchy approach of Robert Gagne (1965). At the conclusion of that paper Shulman raised a provocative question, which we paraphrase as follows: Can the roller coaster of discovery be placed on the well-laid track of a structured curriculum?

Both guided discovery and the ACE-cycle make effective use of small groups of students working together to explore mathematical ideas. These explorations lead to learning, and since the students have taken an active role in these acquisitions, they tend to possess their newly acquired knowledge at a deeper level. Students understand more completely and remember better the ideas that they have acquired when taking an active role in explorations of a mathematical concept.

Depending on their philosophy of teaching and learning mathematics and on the needs and/or learning styles of the students, good instructors make a variety of instructional decisions. In this chapter, we will first discuss the model of guided discovery learning in small groups, which we define as students working together to establish or develop mathematical results that are new to them. These results need not be original discoveries new to the mathematics profession, but the results are new to the students who discover them. Since guided discovery is compatible with any of the last three views of learning from the previous chapter, the aims of the instructor, in terms of how he views mathematics and learning, will have an effect on the structure and content of any guided discovery activity. Next we will compare guided discovery and the ACE-cycle by presenting perspectives from instructors who are using each of these models in making decisions about what they teach and how to teach it. We will also present a perspective of the teacher's role in group learning and an example of Socratic dialogue. Finally, there is a section on active learning strategies in a group context and suggestions for further research. As instructors reflect on their own beliefs about the nature of mathematics, these complementary perspectives give them some options on which to base pedagogical decisions. They may choose one of these paradigms, another perspective, or a hybrid of the forms under consideration.

In the context of a structured curriculum, students function in a manner similar to mathematicians, but they follow a mathematical trail that has been laid out for them in advance by their instructors. Students operate as mathematical investigators in a domain where the major pathways and signposts are offered to them by the curriculum through a system of situations to explore, examples to consider, and propositions to state and prove.

Historical Perspective

Teaching strategies that involve students in explorations or investigations (Bruner, 1960; Polya, 1962, 1965; Shulman, 1968) have recently assumed new importance in the context of the reform movement within the mathematics education profession. The main assumption behind these strategies is that learning a particular subject can be accomplished more fruitfully if the student is actively involved in explorations that lead her toward discovery of ideas or in investigations that encourage her to construct new mental images to fit observations made while engaged in these activities. In this way, the student is discovering or constructing his own knowledge rather than accepting ideas from others through direct instruction or rote learning. The instructor's role in guided discovery learning consists of creating favorable conditions for the moments of discovery. This technique succeeds as an instructional tool because the process of discovering knowledge offers students both enjoyment and a mental exercise that is of lasting quality. The discovery method of presenting mathematical knowledge has a long history. Huygens says: "...that which comes first and which matters most is the way in which the discovery has been made. It is this knowledge which gives most satisfaction and which one requires from discoverers. It seems therefore, preferable to supply the idea through which the result first came to light and through which it will be most readily understood." Clearly Huygens sees the discovery method as leading the learner through the historical path of discovery.

The discovery approach to teaching relies on designing situations and using techniques that allow the student to participate in the discovery of mathematical knowledge. The teacher can facilitate a student's movement along the path of discovery, but ultimately the student has to make the discovery by herself. The discovery method can be utilized in various learning environments including instructor-student interaction, cooperative learning, or individual discovery requiring intensive, isolated work followed by sharing results in class.

The term *discovery* was used as far back as the fourteenth century. In this century, there are at least three approaches to guided discovery learning in collegiate mathematics.

1. George Polya (1962, 1965) described numerous heuristic problem strategies in his

many books on problem solving and discovery learning. These heuristic processes are often used in Socratic discovery learning dialogues conducted by the teacher with a class of students. The processes can also be used for individual or small-group problem solving and discovery. Polya's work has led to considerable research on heuristic strategies by Schoenfeld (1985) and many other investigators.

2. The highly competitive, individual discovery approach of R. L. Moore has been used mostly in the field of point set topology. Without talking to anyone else or reading any books, students are expected to prove theorems or construct counterexamples. Students who believe they have solved a problem present their results to the class for discussion and critique. A number of outstanding point-set topologists began their work in graduate school by learning via the Moore method. Moise (1965), commenting on this method, pointed out that despite the apparent slowness of the method, "knowledge gained in this manner has power far out of proportion to its quantity."

3. Neil Davidson (1971) designed the small-group discovery method to maintain much of the intellectual challenge of the Moore method but to change the social conditions and to build success for a wider range of students. In Davidson's approach, students work together in small groups to perform mathematical tasks such as solving problems or proving theorems. Weissglass (1990) developed a small-group laboratory approach in his courses in mathematics for elementary school teachers. The students work together, typically in groups of four members, with basic guidelines for sharing the leadership of the group, achieving a single group solution, and assuring that everyone in the group understands the solution.

Small-Group Discovery in Abstract Algebra

One specific example of an entire mathematics curriculum designed for small-group discovery learning is the text *Abstract Algebra: An Active Learning Approach* by Davidson and Gulick (1976). Students consider numerous specific examples of mathematical systems, such as groups,

rings, integral domains, or fields. They work out all the details to show that these systems do or do not satisfy the appropriate axioms. Examples considered include a large variety of sets of real numbers, complex numbers, matrices of small dimensions such as 2×2, permutations, symmetries of geometrical figures, and integers modulo n with appropriate operations on these sets. No theorems are proved in the text; students construct all proofs working together in their small groups. For example, an important question for investigation is the relationship between the number of elements in a subgroup of a finite group and the number of elements in the whole group. Students begin by finding all the subgroups of the groups of integers modulo n under addition, where n ranges from 2 to 12. They examine the patterns and relationships that emerge in the data, and readily conjecture that the number of elements, *i.e.*, the order, of the subgroup divides the order of the finite group. Thus they conjecture Lagrange's theorem.

The students do the proof of Lagrange's theorem. First, they work with the concept of a coset of a subgroup and consider examples of cosets. Recall that for a subgroup H of a group G, the left coset of H determined by an element a in G is defined as follows: $aH = \{ah : h \in H\}$. For specific subgroups of the integers modulo 6, the set $\{0, 1, 2, 3, 4, 5\}$ under addition, students find all left cosets by computation. For example, students find the distinct cosets of the subgroup $\{0, 3\}$ to be $\{0, 3\}$, $\{1, 4\}$, and $\{2, 5\}$. They investigate questions from the text such as the following (with student responses given in brackets):

- Are all (or any) cosets also subgroups of the integers modulo 6? [Yes, but the only coset that is a subgroup is the original subgroup $\{0, 3\}$.]

- Is every element of the group in some left coset? [Yes.]

- Can two different elements determine the same left coset? [Yes, for example 1 and 4 both determine the same coset $\{1, 4\}$.]

- Do two different left cosets have any common elements? [No, if the cosets are different, they do not overlap.]

- How many different left cosets of the subgroup are there? [3.]

- How many elements are in each left coset? [2, which is the number of elements in the subgroup.]

- What is the relationship between the order of the group, the order of the subgroup, and the number of distinct left cosets? [$6 = 2 \times 3$. In words, the order of the group is equal to the product of the order of the subgroup and the number of distinct left cosets.]

This sequence of questions then becomes the sequence of the usual lemmas that aid in the proof of Lagrange's theorem. Students prove all lemmas by working together cooperatively. In essence, they end up proving that the distinct left cosets of a subgroup form a partition of the finite group, *i.e.,* a collection of mutually disjoint nonempty subsets whose union is the whole group. They use this to prove that the order of the group is equal to the product of the order of the subgroup and the number of distinct left cosets. The logic of the entire sequence of lemmas becomes clear when students first consider particular, concrete examples and then find the general proofs. Some groups of students need only to consider one specific example, such as the integers modulo 6 with its subgroups and related cosets; other student groups prefer to look at an additional example, such as the integers modulo 12.

Note that the sequence of steps in the development and proof of Lagrange's theorem departs from the traditional pattern of definition, theorem, and proof. All these elements eventually appear, but in an atmosphere rich in consideration of specific examples that then lead to conjectures and eventually to proofs. In this manner, students working together in small groups can develop and prove all the theorems in a first course in abstract algebra. Students consider and work out the details for a variety of examples, formulate conjectures, and provide either proofs or counterexamples to those conjectures. While the overall structure and sequence of the course are provided by the text, students experience a strong sense of exploration, engagement, and discovery as they work through a sequence of examples, definitions, conjectures, problems, theorems, proofs, and sometimes counterexamples during each day of the course.

Developing Curriculum Materials for Guided Discovery

Developing full-scale curriculum materials for intensive small-group problem solving through guided discovery is a challenging task that requires repeated trials and refinements of the materials. This can sometimes take several years, as was the case for the abstract algebra development. To streamline this process, a procedure for curriculum construction with student input was developed by Davidson, McKeen, and Eisenberg (1973). They worked with one student group at a time outside of class, carefully observed their responses to a proposed set of curriculum materials, and revised the activities and questions based on observation and feedback. This process was repeated with another group, and it allowed for repeated cycles of trial and revision within each semester. By involving groups of students in the development of activities, the researchers were able to incorporate students' perspectives in the curriculum. With small incentives, it is usually possible to find several groups of students willing to participate in this process in any given semester. Students are often delighted to have a chance to advise faculty about the best ways to design the tasks and activities.

Many faculty members do not have the time, energy, or inclination toward major curriculum development efforts. Because of the reform efforts in mathematics, more curriculum materials that make substantial use of small-group learning are now becoming available. As an alternative, faculty can choose to switch back and forth between brief lectures and short activities for pairs or groups. Doing so typically involves a trade-off between discovery and coverage of material. We find that developing brief tasks or learning activities for groups is not nearly as demanding as developing a full-scale curriculum of activities for small-group discovery.

The ACE-Cycle in Developmental and College Algebra Courses

Betty Rogers is an experienced instructor who had recognized the value of discovery learning for students, but who maintained for many years that this method of instruction was entirely too time consuming. Even guided discovery seemed an unattainable objective with the time constraints imposed by required syllabi in a course such as college algebra. However, as she began using a form of cooperative learning that was based on the ACE-cycle in her classes, she observed that her students understood mathematical concepts at a level higher than they had previously. As students worked together on specified class activities, they seemed better prepared for the class discussions and mini-lectures that followed these activities.

Activities in the ACE-cycle are often posed in ways that raise questions and allow the student to choose an approach to solving the problem. As students recognize there is an overriding principle to be found among the problems, they sometimes withdraw briefly from the group to reflect and use individual strategies. Some students reach for calculators while others approach the problem with pencil and paper to begin writing and sketching. Individuals then introduce ideas to the group for reinforcement, clarification, or discussion. Ultimately, the dynamics of group interaction help the students to combine the individual ideas into a cohesive entity.

The students are expected to consider in depth the problems posed in the activities. Working together in cooperative groups provides social support for investigating problems whose solutions are not as readily obtained as solutions in previous courses. Since the objective of the activities is to think deeply about some ideas, the students derive much of the benefit of the investigations even if they do not completely solve the problems that are posed as activities. The class discussion that follows brings out the concepts even if the students have not fully discovered them. Betty Rogers has found that the ACE-cycle, even though it poses challenging problems for student investigation, is a particularly successful strategy for students in both her developmental and college algebra courses. Many of these students were less successful in high school mathematics courses than their peers who placed directly into calculus. Students who take developmental or college algebra often approach these courses with an intrinsic fear of mathematics, which has been developed and amplified since early elementary school. The unfamiliar notation and more abstract concepts of algebra compound earlier mathematics anxieties.

Working in groups seems to alleviate much of the anxiety related to algebra. Students express the sentiment that collaborative efforts of the group help them to understand the concepts and, more importantly, eliminate threatening feelings of isolation that previously plagued their attempts at mathematics. Even students who at first are reluctant to participate in the groups find the activities helpful and become active contributors.

This method is particularly successful in extended-length evening classes. Some of Rogers' classes meet once a week for four and one-half hours, and many of the students in these classes are non-traditional students who come to class after having worked an eight-hour day. These students often approach their mathematics classes with supper in their hands and fear in their eyes. Not knowing anyone else in the class, they feel particularly isolated.

To eliminate some of the feeling of aloneness and to allow the students to get to know each other, the first class session begins with an icebreaker. One of the favorite opening exercises is a variation of the three-step interview (Kagan, 1992). The class is divided into pairs with none of the partners knowing each other. They are instructed to interview each other for three minutes apiece, to learn not just name, major, and hometown, but "something that I would not know about the person if I read his admission and advisement files." The shared information is often fascinating, and it frequently establishes common bonds among class members. One evening, for example, two students who had never met learned that their fathers were both employed by NASCAR teams.

In-class groups may be formed arbitrarily by such attributes as birth month or random selection. Sometimes groups are formed by such homogeneous characteristics as grade level (early childhood, middle grades, or special education) that prospective teachers aspire to teach. In evening classes where students may live 50 to 100 miles away from campus, students may form different groups that can meet conveniently for out-of-class assignments and projects.

In a typical class period, Rogers begins by giving a brief introduction to the evening's topic, and then she assigns a set of problems related to that specific topic. Working in groups, the students generate solutions to these examples by any appropriate method. At first, the students may generate solutions by trial and error. After solving several problems, they begin to recognize patterns and are able to generalize methods of solution. In both developmental algebra and college algebra,

Rogers has students use relatively concrete procedures and talk to each other about the methodology they are using. These in-class activities lead students to verbalize more abstract concepts or to formulate procedures for solving equations. Some groups may be asked to present their ideas for the whole class. Rogers concludes the class by summarizing the concepts.

After several class periods, permanent in-class groups are formed, each group chooses a team name, and each member of the group is assigned a number. This allows for activities to be approached using a variation of Kagan's numbered heads procedure (1992). Each group is given a different set of problems to solve. After the groups have solved their problems, students are called on by team name and number, *e.g.,* Experts #2, to demonstrate their problem and solution on the chalkboard. Thus, students realize that all members of the group must be able to explain each problem that they have solved. Daily grades for classwork or homework may be assigned by randomly taking one paper from each group. Since the students never know whose paper will be selected, the group is conscientious in seeing that everyone has completed the assignment.

Various activities are used to engage students in solving problems and discussing the strategies for solution with the others in their groups. For example, each group may be asked to create several equations within specific guidelines of difficulty (say, equations with coefficients that are fractions or decimals), and then work out the solutions for this set of equations. The problem sets are randomly distributed to other groups. If a group is unable to solve the problems they receive, the originating group must be prepared to give hints or to demonstrate a solution. This requirement helps to avoid the construction of tedious and unusually difficult problems.

In another activity, the instructor writes equations that require multiple steps to solve on different panels of the board. There should be the same number of equations as there are student groups. Each group is given a different color of chalk or marker and instructed to work one step of solving an equation. Then the groups rotate to the next equation. A different person is responsible for recording the thinking of the group for each step in the rotation. The process continues until the equations are solved and checked. This method can

be altered for a large class by writing the problems on paper, providing the groups with pens of different colors and passing the papers from group to group. This procedure is particularly successful since students not only solve the problem but also must consider the previous operations. They are forced to look for mistakes and to consider alternative methods of solution. The various colors provide a sense of ownership. When the solutions are complete, the student groups might be asked to write out a set of general methods for solving problems of this type, or the groups might be divided into pairs with each person interviewing the other to generate solution patterns. For example, students might say "simplify each side of the equation," "aim to get the variables on one side and the constants on the other," and so on.

An important topic of algebra is the solution of quadratic equations. Students taught by a traditional lecture method frequently are able to solve an equation when the method is specified, but they may have difficulty in choosing among the various methods. After the students have had some practice with several methods of solving quadratic equations (factoring, the quadratic formula, and completing the square), carefully selected equations that can be solved by more than one method are written on the chalk board or on sheets of paper. Each group receives an equation to solve by any method of the members' choosing. Then the next group must select another method of solution. When the equations have been solved by all possible methods, a final group selects the method that they think is most appropriate for the specific equation. One student presents the group's conclusion and reasons to the class. This activity gives students practice with the various methods, and it helps them to see the relationship among the alternative methods. After this activity, the students have a better understanding of the idea that one method of solution may be more appropriate than other methods for a particular problem.

In group contexts as well as in individual work, it is important to differentiate between the students who are seeking help because of time constraints or lack of group effort and the students who have actually reached a point where the material is beyond their grasp. Certain topics seem to confound even the most diligent and explorative of groups, and Rogers finds that she sometimes needs to provide explanations or give direct instruction on particular concepts. For example, the idea that the logarithm of the product of numbers equals the sum of the logarithms of the numbers may elude the students even though they have worked a large number of examples. Rogers might offer suggestions as she moves around the room from one group to another, or she may give a brief lecture if all the groups seem to have difficulty formulating the same idea.

During a typical class activity, students make some errors. However, there tend to be fewer mistakes when groups generate solutions because the students check each other's work. When problems are presented on the board, the students are asked to consider the solutions of the other groups and to identify any solutions that seem incorrect. The class then discusses where the error occurred and how it could be corrected. In this way, errors can be used to enhance instruction without attaching "blame" to one student in particular.

After using cooperative learning for several years, Rogers is convinced that students can move through the required course material with less hesitancy and that they are more articulate in their answers. She is able to pace the material so that the required syllabus is covered. The students' increased feelings of self-confidence allow them to be more adventurous and creative in their solutions. The cooperative environment creates an encouraging class atmosphere where everyone is willing to contribute. The students seem to actually enjoy classes that they only expected to tolerate, and her course evaluations from the students reflect this positive attitude.

The Instructor's Role in Group Learning

The instructor in group learning situations is concerned with designing situations that encourage group interaction and with facilitating the thought processes of students. To accomplish this skillfully, the teacher needs both knowledge and understanding of the dimensions of the students' cognition. He listens carefully to the students and tries to understand the routes and the processes of each student's thinking with regard to problems. In preparing for class, the instructor must pay careful attention to the design of activities, the selection and sequencing of examples, and the scope and challenge of the task. On the other hand, there can be a spontaneous introduction of an issue or question arising from an unexpected approach that a student takes to a problem. By entering into unplanned spontaneous dialogs with individual students and groups, as well as by presenting problems that have been carefully structured and sequenced, instructors and students enter into a new type of thinking partnership. The instructor provides professional understanding of the process of teaching and learning and a clear idea of the instructional goals and expectations for the students while still remaining open to the reality of what actually transpires in the classroom.

In contemporary mathematics classrooms, there are many ways in which dialogue may occur. A whole-class Socratic dialogue using the heuristic strategies of Polya (1962, 1965) can be planned. Small-group discovery strategies can be used in conjunction with cooperative learning (Davidson, 1971, 1990). Individuals and small groups can be interviewed by techniques similar to those used by researchers to probe the structure of the learner's thinking. Some Socratic dialogues may occur spontaneously as the fragment below illustrates.

Bronislaw Czarnocha teaches intermediate algebra to students who speak English as a second language. His class provides opportunities to engage students in a deeper level of thinking and to observe them in the act of constructing a new understanding of an idea or concept. This example of an interchange between Czarnocha and his student occurred during a discussion of the domain of the function $f(x) = \sqrt{x}$. Similar discussions would be possible with groups of students.

Czarnocha: "Can all real values of x be used for the domain of the function $f(x) = \sqrt{x+3}$?"

Student: "No, negative x's cannot be used."

Czarnocha: "How about $x = -5$?"

Student: "No good."

Czarnocha: "How about $x = -4$?"

Student: "No good either."

Czarnocha: "How about $x = -3$?"

Student, after a minute of thought: "It works here."

Czarnocha: "How about $x = -2$?"

Student: "It works here too."

A moment later she adds: "Those x's which are smaller than -3 can't be used here."

Czarnocha: "Right. How about $\sqrt{x+5}$?"

Student: "x's smaller than -5 can't be used."

Czarnocha: "How about $\sqrt{x-1}$?"

Student, after a minute of thought: "Smaller than 1 can't be used."

A traditional way of dealing with the confusion exhibited by this student might have been to provide immediately a counterexample to the student's original answer, or to explain that what was needed here was the solution of the inequality: $x+3>0$. The spontaneous questioning route taken by this teacher has not only shown the student her thinking error, but it also led the student towards that moment of silent reflection where a small cognitive reorganization of her thinking took place. The examples that followed were designed to convince both the student and the teacher that the reorganization had become stable and could be applied or transferred to other situations.

In this episode, Czarnocha employed simple guided questioning while asking the student to examine particular numerical examples. Within his questioning, he was deliberately creating Piaget's discomfort or disequilibrium. This contrasts with the small-group approach to guided discovery in the way that the examples are used. In guided discovery, the teacher builds examples for students to consider, and the students themselves select the numbers to test in the problem conditions. This method can be used either in groups of four or with partners, as in the Think-Pair-Share procedure.

Active Learning Strategies in a Group Context

Mathematics is often a barrier that discourages students, especially minorities and women, from making an ambitious career choice. Recent initiatives in mathematics and statistics play a crucial role in strengthening mathematics and statistical education at all levels, and hence in assuring that more students will succeed.

Martha Aliaga teaches a statistics class designed to provide an overview of the field of statistics. Even in large classes of 175 students, she begins forming groups on the first day. The instructor attaches a number to each chair with numbers ranging from one to the maximum number of students in the class. As students enter the room, they receive a slip of paper with a number and are instructed to sit in the seat with the corresponding number. The instructor then points out the partners (groups of two) who will work together for the first class.

The partners then introduce themselves through exercises, and they exchange phone numbers. The following day students are invited to change seats if they prefer, but the majority usually chooses to continue with the original partners. Students are also encouraged to work together on homework. The environment is conducive to learning as well as enjoyment. When necessary for certain statistics problems, two pairs can be combined to form a group of four. In smaller classes, with 20 or so students, Aliaga uses groups of four. In both large and small classes, the pairs or groups become a support group or association group. Although this support is valuable for all students, it is especially important for minority students who feel isolated in a majority-white institution.

Aliaga always personalizes her classes, no matter how large, by walking all around the room, getting close to the students, and asking them questions. As the students start to respond she walks farther away from them so they have to speak more loudly and then the whole class is able to hear them. Her students are not afraid to ask questions, even in a large class. She tells her students, "I will pose many questions, and I will invite you to make mistakes. Your mistakes will help not only you but also other students to understand better. Your confusion is good, it is a tool to help me teach." She can say, "Good, that is a great mistake. It shows me what I didn't explain clearly." In her classroom, mistakes are welcomed as an aid to her teaching.

The university specifies the curriculum, and Aliaga must cover the syllabus. However, she can use any effective teaching plan and implement those strategies that best guide her students toward integration of their knowledge. She respects their needs and the pace at which they can understand new ideas. Each semester she has a different group of students and must again create an environment that engages her students in the course content and leads them to learn statistics.

Aliaga carefully structures her syllabus so that the important content of statistics that she must cover during the course is offered to the students at a pace that meets their ability to learn new ideas. As their knowledge-base increases, she can move faster and in larger conceptual blocks. She often tries to find situations that surprise the students, believing that paradoxes are an effective tool for teaching. For example, students may add percentages in situations where it makes no sense to do so. However, they will remember later the striking situations where the class made this mistake.

The way a problem is presented is crucial. Aliaga uses two overhead projectors when the class is large. One projector displays the problem under consideration. This problem is presented in big letters with no more than four lines so everyone can see the problem and refer back to it. The other projector is used for discussion of the solution, related examples, *etc.* A graphing calculator can also be displayed on the second overhead, so that the whole class can see the calculations that lead to a solution. In large classes, students talk with their partners and offer suggestions that the instructor demonstrates on the calculator or writes on the overhead transparency.

It is important for the instructor to build time into the class session for students to work with their groups or partners to complete some of the problems for themselves. Sometimes, when Aliaga notices that she wants to help the students too much and finds herself answering too many of their questions, thereby depriving them of the opportunity to think through the situation by themselves, she leaves the room for a few minutes "for a cup of coffee." Bruffee (1993) suggests this practice of leaving the room at strategically chosen moments in his approach to collaborative learning. University students can be left alone in the classroom briefly, and they will work intensely without close supervision. When she returns to the class, many of the problems have been resolved. This is part of giving power to the students.

Aliaga tries to build her classes on what the students have already studied and attempted to solve for homework. Before class, the students write on the board the problems that they could not solve by themselves or with their group members. When Aliaga arrives in the classroom, the problem statements are already written on the board. Sometimes she leaves the room again, saying, "Someone is calling me. I will come back in a few minutes." By the time she returns all the problems have been solved without her input!

The students debate with and question each other to arrive at correct solutions. The group must share, discuss, and agree on their combined answer, which then is presented as the group's proposed response to the problem. The group must review the statistical principles involved over and over, thus learning them more fully, as they try to convince the other group members to accept their suggested answers. When a group or individual student poses questions, the instructor redirects the questions to the remainder of the class. There is a variety of methods to enable students to depend on their own understanding and abilities to find a solution. The class can be used to expand the student's awareness of resources other than the teacher. Should no one have the answer, the instructor provides it or provides a source to find it. The students are encouraged to participate, to talk, to debate, to disagree, and to argue.

Students must be tested on material while still at the beginning of the learning curve so that errors can be noted immediately and corrected before they become an erroneous part of their statistical thinking and understanding. Aliaga's quizzes test all previous material with emphasis on the most current. This approach avoids the feeling that all previous assumptions about statistics are to be forgotten and that class starts over with each new unit.

In many universities, students evaluate all faculty members at the end of the course. Aliaga does not find this helpful since the class is finished by the time she gets the data. Hence, in addition to the end-of-semester evaluations, she does assessments using evaluation forms that students fill out every Friday immediately after they finish their quiz. This gives her feedback each week that she uses to make decisions about what happens next. Throughout the semester, she makes frequent adjustments based on student feedback.

Aliaga believes that students can achieve and that they can learn difficult material successfully. She believes that students enter the university intending to succeed. She tells them: "My role in this class is not as judge, not to fail you, but as a facilitator of your success." She strives to make her examinations difficult since she believes students want to be challenged. She sees her position as instructor as an opportunity to prepare students to meet this level of challenge.

Some Questions for Research

There are several open questions for those who are interested in the development of effective class activities for use with either the discovery technique or the A-phase of the ACE-cycle. One problem is how to make the knowledge gained during the investigative processes a long-lasting feature of the student 's cognitive apparatus. A related issue, and possible solution, is the degree to which combining investigations with the processes of verbalization through discussion and writing increases students' abstract understanding and their ability to use the formal language and structures of mathematics. For example, how do students learn to write good mathematical proofs?

There are indications that a combination of small-group discussion and individual writing activities may be effective teaching strategies. In the "Model for Learning and Teaching Mathematics" Steffe and Smock (1975) propose a "carefully arranged interplay between spoken words which symbolize a mathematical concept and the set of actions performed in the process of constructing a tangible representation of the concept." They recommend that a "mathematical vocabulary should be developed ... to explicate and provide embodiments for the concept." Czarnocha (1999) sees writing as a means to overcome what he considers a fundamental weakness of the discovery technique. He thinks that the difficulty lies not in the facilitation of the conceptual discovery but in the translation of that discovery into a precise, formal mathematical concept. There seems to be a significant gap between the intuitive conceptual understanding derived from the accumulation of concrete experiences and formulation of the mathematical concept. Hendrix (1961) addresses nonverbal awareness in discovery.

This is possibly the same shortcoming that has undermined the effectiveness of the traditional approach. Here however, we observe it from the opposite end. In the traditional approach, an instructor may introduce a formal concept through a carefully planned lecture; a number of illustrations and examples may be offered that, it is hoped, relate the new material to the students' current state of knowledge. Difficulties are encountered during this process of relating; there is a gap between the formal aspect of the new concept that is being presented and the concrete aspect of students' state of knowledge. As a result, the students' efforts may focus on the match between a problem and a multitude of formal rules rather than on understanding. Confusion and disenchantment follow.

Investigative approaches, which are used by both the ACE-cycle and the discovery method, encounter the same difficulties, but from the other side. The student works with a number of examples that have been carefully constructed and sequenced to challenge the student's present state of knowledge and to lead the student to formulate a new or modified mental image or to adopt a new language that corresponds to a particular insight. This fits with Bruner's (1971) notion of inactive, iconic, and symbolic phases in the learning of a concept or principle.

It seems that an emphasis on verbalization of the thought processes might lead towards bridging the gap between the formal aspect of the new concept to be learned and the learner's current understanding of that concept. Verbalization occurs naturally in cooperative small-group discussions, where students articulate their thinking and reasoning, ask each other questions, challenge others' reasoning, offer alternative approaches, and provide detailed explanations. The introduction of writing into mathematics classes strengthens this verbalization further. Students' ability to write about their thinking in mathematics is enhanced by the opportunity to talk about their ideas first with their group members. Hence, one powerful sequence is group discussion of mathematics followed by writing about the mathematics discussed. (See Think-Share-Write in Chapter 3.) What is meant here is not necessarily a journal or descriptive writing, but using writing to express clearly the intuitive ideas and concepts that appear during "Aha!" moments of sudden insight or discovery.

Hadamard (1945) discusses at length mathematical invention and discovery by mathematicians. He describes the work done by students in mathematics classes: "Between the work of the student who tries to solve a problem in geometry or algebra and a work of invention, one can say that there is only a difference of degree, a difference of level, both works being of a similar nature." Hadamard (1945) proposes four chronological stages in the process of creation: preparation, incubation, illumination, and verification. Much of this he attributes to Poincaré. The stages are:

1.   *Preparation:* You work hard on a problem, giving your conscious attention to it.

2.   *Incubation:* Your conscious preparation sets in motion an unconscious mechanism that searches for the solution. Poincaré wrote that ideas are like the hooked atoms of Epicurus: preparation sets them in motion and they continue their dance during incubation. The unconscious mechanism evaluates the resulting combination on aesthetic criteria; most of them are useless.

3.   *Illumination:* An idea that satisfies your unconscious criteria suddenly emerges into your consciousness.

4.   *Verification:* You carry out further conscious work in order to verify your illumination, to formulate it more precisely, and perhaps to follow up on its consequences.

Given these stages, an interesting distinction emerges between discovery-oriented activities designed to be done in class and those designed to be done out of class. Activities intended to lead to discovery in class cannot be based on an extended period of incubation; there is not adequate time for it during class. Hence, activities intended for in-class guided discovery are typically designed so that illumination or insight can occur within a reasonably short time frame. This requires guidance by either the activity itself or by the instructor through careful selection and sequencing of examples, breaking large investigations down into smaller component parts, or judicious use of directions or hints. Activities requiring longer incubation time might begin in class and then continue with group meetings outside class. Alternatively, a major activity can be spread over several class periods.

Conclusion

Dubinsky's ACE-cycle and Davidson's discovery learning provide the framework for a variety of cooperative learning experiences. However, each instructor must adapt these pedagogical concepts to her own teaching style, the demands of the curriculum, and the learning styles of the students. In this chapter, we have presented discussions of both the ACE-cycle and discovery learning. These discussions were followed by examples from experienced instructors using these modes of instruction. We have also included examples of teaching with Socratic dialog and active learning utilizing small groups. Ultimately, each instructor may choose one of these paradigms, an appropriate combination of forms, or an alternative approach that will be consistent with her philosophy of teaching and the needs of the students.

Chapter 7

Spreading the Word:
Designing and Presenting Workshops

Anne Brown, Neil A. Davidson, and Elizabeth C. Rogers

Introduction

This chapter is intended to serve two purposes. Our main purpose is to provide basic outlines that can be adapted by presenters to design their own workshops on cooperative learning. At the same time, the design of each outline has at its core the intent to create a cooperative atmosphere in the proposed workshops, so our suggestions can also be interpreted more generally as suggestions for establishing a cooperative classroom.

The chapter is divided into three main parts. The first section provides outlines of introductory workshops on cooperative learning that can be completed in one half-day, in one hour, and in two hours. In addition there is an outline for presenting a four-hour workshop for experienced users of cooperative learning. The second section provides details of the procedures and strategies used in the workshop outlines, while the third section contains some helpful hints for successful workshop presentation.

Workshop Outlines

In each case, the outline as presented here is brief. Additional information on many of the aspects of the workshop outlines is given in the following section.

A plan for structuring a half-day workshop

1. Give a brief introduction.
   a) What is cooperative learning?
   b) What will happen during the workshop?
2. Establish a cooperative climate using one or two icebreakers, such as having participants all shake hands and then line up according to the number of years they have taught or used cooperative learning.
3. Place the participants in groups.

   Participants might be grouped according to the course in which they are most likely to use cooperative learning; you may find it helpful to collect this information prior to the workshop if possible. Another possibility is to group participants in a way that ensures that a variety of levels of experience are present in each group. The icebreaker mentioned in B can be used as a basis for forming groups in this way. Finally, you may also want to take this opportunity to mention some of the other methods discussed below for forming groups in classroom.

4. Use one or more team-building activities.

   Help the workshop teams build *esprit de corps* by using a team-building activity such as the Three-Step Interview (see Chapter 3). For the workshop, it might be helpful to focus the interview on eliciting participants' past experiences with using cooperative learning.

5. Focus on building skills with easy structures.

We advise spending the major portion of the workshop on this activity, unless the participants have extensive prior experience. Here are some issues to consider in designing this portion of the workshop.

a) Some of the easiest structures are Think-Pair-Share, Roundtable, Numbered-Heads Reporting, and Pairs-Check.

b) Include an opportunity for participants to reflect on their experiences with these procedures and activities, and then report to the whole group. One way to do this is to ask each reporter to give one new observation per group.

c) Since it is not possible to do activities using all the easy structures during the workshop, the leader might describe others at this point or provide a handout with additional information.

d) Conclude with an activity in which each group generates example activities for each of the strategies mentioned. One possibility is to use Jigsaw (see Chapter 3), where each Expert group tries to generate example activities for one of the easy structures, which members then present to their Home groups.

6. Discuss participants' concerns regarding the implementation of cooperative learning.

a) Have groups discuss issues with one member recording concerns and then follow up with a large-group discussion.

b) In our experience, some of the most frequently mentioned concerns are those in the following list. (Detailed information about these concerns appears in Chapters 2, 3, and 4.)

i) Assessment concerns (formative and summative)

ii) Problems with group dynamics

iii) Students who refuse to participate or cooperate and/or students who are left out of group processes

iv) The coverage problem, *i.e.,* needing to complete a required syllabus or amount of material

v) Difficult seating arrangements

vi) Size of class and size of groups

vii) Providing a convincing rationale for using cooperative learning strategies

c) It can be helpful to follow up by presenting the participants with a case study involving some of their concerns and having groups brainstorm solutions.

7. In closing, facilitate a cooperative review of the main points of the workshop with the aim of having participants develop their own action plan for getting started on implementing cooperative learning strategies.

A plan for structuring a one-hour presentation

The purpose is to inspire people to begin to use cooperative learning strategies in their teaching. The only feasible goal is to increase their awareness about cooperative learning, since it is practically impossible to build skills in only one hour. Such a presentation might be titled "A Taste of Cooperative Learning". Here is one way to structure it.

1. Introduction.

a) Tell success stories, including examples from the classroom.

b) Show pictures of cooperative settings on the overhead.

2. Engage participants in two to four simple activities that use the easier strategies, such as Think-Pair-Share and Roundtable.

3. Provide commentary that relates participants' experiences with the strategies during this session to what happens in classroom implementation.

4. Summarize the major points of the presentation, being sure to include some discussion of why instructors are often reluctant to try cooperative learning (see the concerns listed in the previous plan).

5. Close by reassuring participants that many people have become successful at using cooperative learning strategies through implementing them one step at a time.

A plan for structuring a two-hour presentation

A presentation of this length can include some skill building. The suggested breakdown of time is 1. 25 hours of activities and . 75 hours of overview via lecture, whole-class discussion, and responses to questions. Use the same basic format as the one-hour presentation, but augment it with some of the components from the half-day workshop outline.

A plan for structuring a four-hour presentation for experienced participants

Barbara Reynolds and Bill Fenton developed this plan for a workshop presented at the Toronto MathFest in 1998. The workshop was presented on two days, in two two-hour sessions. Each strategy mentioned is mentioned in Chapter 3, unless indicated otherwise.

Session 1

1. Activities for the first 50 minutes.

    a) Set up pairs by a method that encourages diversity within pairs.

       i) Work a short exercise requiring pairs

       ii) Use Think-Pair-Share to ask for responses

    b) Create groups of four by pairing pairs.

       i) Work a more involved example that will require more heads to think about it

       ii) Have groups share and critique responses with another group

    c) Use Think-Group-Share (a variant of Think-Pair-Share) to reflect on the group dynamics.

       i) Why did the pairs get the shorter problem?

       ii) Why did larger group get the second problem?

       iii) How did you work on the problems? What kinds of interaction happened within your group?

    d) Lead a brief group discussion in which participants consider how these examples might be used in the courses they teach.

2. Activities for the next 55 minutes.

    a) Randomly select new groups using a deck of cards.

    b) Solve a more complicated problem using Triptych (see Chapter 3 for some possible choices of a problem).

    c) Use Numbered-Heads Reporting to reflect on the group process.

    d) Discuss issues of assessment. Use Roundtable in the groups and then Numbered-Heads Reporting. Main issues are:

       i) Individual versus group assessment

       ii) Group rewards

       iii) Individual accountability

       iv) Encouraging cooperation while ensuring individual accountability

3. Activities for the final 15 minutes.

    a) Have participants complete a questionnaire providing information that can be used to form groups for the second session. Ask them to identify courses in which they might use cooperative learning strategies so that implementation issues can be discussed in the context of specific courses during the second session.

    b) Hand out the homework assignment—a collection of short readings that can be read overnight. Also distribute a one-page, very brief description of some easy-to-use strategies, including those used in the first session.

Session 2

1. Activities for the first 45 minutes.

    a) Assign groups based on questionnaire responses. Individuals sit at tables where they find their name on a group list.

    b) Discuss the handout on classroom strategies with their groups.

    c) Use Think-Pair-Share to report out the discussion.

    d) Ask participants to identify strategies that they have observed thus far in the workshop. Which strategies did they recognize?

e) Discuss issues raised by the assigned readings—build a list of issues from participant contributions and, if necessary, raise additional issues to spark discussions.

2. Activities for next 45 minutes.

a) Ask participants to create an activity that they might use in one of their own classes.

b) Discuss issues of small-group formation. (Some of these issues are discussed in the assigned readings; see also Chapter 2 of this book.)

    i) Selection methods

    ii) Size of groups

    iii) Permanent versus changing groups

c) Possible problems with groups and ways to avoid them. Use Roundtable to generate a list of problems, and Think-Group-Share for the ensuing discussion.

    i) Value of monitoring the groups

    ii) Whether and when to intervene

3. Activities for the last 30 minutes.

This part of the workshop takes the form of a discussion that encourages participants to reflect on the readings and experiences with cooperative learning. It can be helpful to invite additional colleagues who are experienced users of cooperative learning strategies to mix with the participants. For the most productive discussion, group participants by type of institution, school or class size, or course level. Because the participants also have some experience, the second session can focus on the details of implementation issues, as suggested below.

a) Issues of group formation.

    i) How and when to form groups

    ii) Size of groups

    iii) Heterogeneous versus homogeneous groups

    iv) Informal versus formal groups: short-term versus permanent groups

    v) Interaction within the groups, including conflicts and conflict resolution, problems with dominant students

    vi) Pitfalls

b) Coverage of material.

    i) Course content (concept and skill development)

    ii) Process (problem solving, development of intuition, working well in teams, *etc.*)

c) Teacher role versus teaching functions (see Finkel and Monk, 1993). Shift of responsibility away from teaching, toward learning.

d) Assessment issues (see Chapter 4).

    i) Individual assessment and grades

    ii) Group projects and group grades

    iii) Grading schemes

    iv) Group rewards

    v) Positive interdependence

    vi) Competition versus. cooperation

e) Structuring group activities (see Chapter 3).

    i) Classroom strategies to encourage group work

    ii) Problems for group activities: use context-rich problems, or problems requiring decisions about what data is relevant, what concepts are needed, what process to use in working toward the solution

f) Difference between ACE-cycle model and discovery learning model (see Chapter 6).

g) Special situations.

    i) Very large or small classes

    ii) Commuter students

    iii) Working in a computer lab

Workshop Components

In this section, we offer some ideas for adding detail to the components of the workshop outlines. This summary is not intended to be exhaustive, but should give prospective workshop leaders a place to start in designing their own workshop. The next step in designing a workshop would be to refer to the earlier chapters of this book and to the literature on cooperative learning.

Overall, our philosophy is that we should model in the workshop what the participants might do in their classrooms. This section is not content-specific and therefore can be applied to many subjects and instructional levels.

Creating a Cooperative Climate

This topic is divided into community building and team building. While the participants will likely be predisposed to cooperating, their students will not necessarily come into their classes knowing how to work effectively in groups. Some effort will be needed to help students develop the appropriate skills.

First, icebreakers are helpful to begin the community building. Some examples are:

- Getting to Know You: List topics on a sheet of paper (for example, feelings about dogs or cats, tastes in music). After participants list how they feel about each topic, they try to find someone whose feelings or opinions match their own statement. The object is to get a different person to sign each topic that matches (Roy, 1990).

- Numbered Chairs: Each chair in the room has a number assigned to it. When participants enter the room, each person chooses a number at random from a bag and sits in the corresponding chair. Then provide participants with icebreaking questions—for a workshop, you might have them introduce themselves and tell what courses they teach.

- Knots: A group of about 6–8 people stand in a circle. Each person joins hands with two people who are not standing next to them. The goal is to unravel the knots without letting go and without talking. (While we have used this exercise successfully, the leader should be aware that some might be uncomfortable with this activity because of the possibility of accidental physical contact.)

- Corners: People with specified common interests or characteristics cluster in particular corners of the room for discussion about their topics (Kagan, 1992).

After groups are formed, use at least one team-building activity. A number of appropriate activities are presented in Chapters 2 and 3.

Group Formation

To explore the issue of group formation, the leader might first present a range of methods that can be used to form groups. In a subsequent activity, groups could evaluate the alternatives by considering:

- which methods they might be most comfortable using and why

- which strategies they might try first, and in which classes

- advantages and disadvantages of each alternative in various situations

Many of the issues that will or should arise through these discussions are thoroughly discussed in Chapter 2.

Simple Structures

We advise using easier structures in the early activities of the workshop so that participants see that it is not difficult to get started. This might also help them begin to think about how they might use these strategies in their own classes.

Emphasize the importance of starting students with narrowly focused problems, using the easier strategies first, with a progressive development during the course to more open-ended problems and more complex strategies.

There are numerous cooperative structures. Some of the simpler structures for a classroom, all of which are described carefully in Chapter 3, include:

- Three-Step-Interviews

- Think-Pair-Share or Think-Group-Share

- Roundtable, or Simultaneous Roundtable

- Pairs-Check

- Numbered-Heads Reporting

More Complicated Strategies

If the participants are experienced with cooperative learning or doing well with the basic strategies, you might try an activity using one of these more intricate strategies (see Chapter 3 for specific descriptions of each strategy):

- Flock Around (also known as a Carousel)

- Data Sharing

- Jigsaw

- Triptych
- Group Critique
- Group Exchange

Developing a Rationale

Since becoming skilled users of cooperative learning takes considerable time and effort, one might well ask whether cooperative learning is worth the trouble. Some of the participants in your workshop may have this concern. Consequently, it is wise to have the participants explore and begin to resolve this issue while they still have the support of their group.

We suggest asking groups to use the Roundtable strategy to brainstorm on the following question: Why might you try cooperative learning for at least some of the time in some of your classes?

In preparing the report of ideas:

- Group members review the list, and choose several of their best reasons.

- Each group picks a speaker to present their ideas to the whole group.

- The speakers line up in front of the room, and each gives one item from their list, with no repeats, until everyone has given all their ideas.

If it does not come up during the discussion, it is worth mentioning that, for many instructors, the strongest rationale for using cooperative learning is its apparent effect on students. Students often mention the following as benefits of cooperative learning:

- Feelings of isolation are eased. Students learn that they are not the only ones in the class who are struggling with difficult ideas. This helps develop self-confidence in dealing with mathematical ideas.

- Students tend to enjoy the work more.

- Students find it less intimidating to ask a question of a classmate than of an instructor. Often they will understand a response from a classmate better than that offered by the instructor.

- Cooperative learning prepares students for teamwork on the job.

At this point, one might also give a very brief discussion of the benefits of cooperative learning that have been supported through research.

Some of the benefits include:

- There are positive effects on student achievement and the development of problem-solving and thinking skills.

- Cooperative work fosters the growth of self-confidence or self-esteem.

- Giving explanations during group work is positively related to achievement.

- Students develop useful skills with inter-group relations.

- There is more student accountability and responsibility in cooperative learning.

The research base for cooperative learning is discussed in detail in Chapter 1. Additional information can be found in the research references in the Bibliography.

To sum up, there are many positive research results concerning cooperative learning. Also, there is a broad spectrum of mathematical opportunities for using cooperative learning. Any topic is fair game, and a wide variety of possible strategies are available. Our primary goal is student learning, and cooperative learning encourages, if not forces, students to actively engage in the classroom activities. One of the authors observes that "Cooperative learning keeps kids awake, and if they're awake, they just might learn something." He illustrates this point through the following anecdote. As he walked down the hallways of a high school he was visiting, he observed an interesting pattern. Where teachers were lecturing, he saw students asleep, heads down on the desk, or students staring at the ceiling. In contrast, when he passed classrooms in which cooperative learning was being used, he saw students who were energized, talking, working, and enthusiastic.

Developing Your Own Plan for Getting Started

Near the end of a workshop, the leader may want to facilitate a cooperative review of the workshop, with the goal of helping participants develop an action plan for beginning to use cooperative learning strategies in their own classes. A specific list of two or three things each participant might try should be generated. Experienced participants can describe how they started using cooperative learning. Novices might be encouraged to pick one or two strategies to use exclusively at first, adding more as they and their students become more comfortable.

It might be helpful to have participants consider Davidson's Class Flow Sample as follows, which gives options for implementations. Not all of the choices would be used in every class period.

- Group homework check
- Presentation, including simple structures
- Group discovery or problem solving
- Processing group interaction
- Cooperative review of mathematical learning
- Group homework preparation

One easy way to start using cooperative learning is the See-Saw approach. The idea is to divide the lecture into smaller component parts and alternate these with brief pair or group activities. This model is also called lecturette/groupette. There are three main advantages to using this as an initial approach:

- The smaller tasks given engender growth of confidence, both in the groups and in the instructor.

- It helps keep the groups on task, because the task is smaller and has a single focus.

- The instructor and the students develop a sense of pacing when using group work. Students can be given some of the responsibility by asking them to establish a mechanism for shifting between small-group and whole-group activities.

Finally, have the participant groups brainstorm ways to persevere. Here are some possibilities to consider:

- Set realistic and manageable personal goals. (For example, use one cooperative activity in each class each week.)

- Keep a journal. (What did I do? What happened? How can I make it better next time?)

- Form a faculty support group on using cooperative learning, either within or across disciplines. The members might meet twice a month and discuss their efforts to use cooperative learning and possibly other teaching innovations. This is helpful in brainstorming solutions to problems and in keeping the members working on their teaching: no one will want to admit that they haven't tried anything new since the last meeting!

Principles for Designing Activities

Designing activities is a challenging issue for instructors beginning to use cooperative learning. (See Chapters 3 and 5 for extensive discussion of this issue.) Since it would be difficult for workshop participants to have many ideas regarding this more advanced topic even by the end of the introductory workshop, the workshop leader might have them brainstorm specific action plans based on a list of principles such as the following.

- In designing an activity, first think carefully about your goals. Is it intended to develop skill, foster conceptual growth, encourage assimilation and review, or consider examples and counterexamples? The goal of the activity will have an effect on the choice of strategy.

- Provide very clear, step-by-step instructions, and check that students understand the instructions.

- In many courses (notably the courses for elementary education majors), the form and sequencing of group tasks is critical. In any course where some or most of the students tend to be fearful of mathematics, you should try to meet them where they are. Start with easy strategies and simpler problems with definite, verifiable answers. Over the semester, gradually relax the structure to include more complex strategies and more open-ended problems.

- Aimless exploration is often unproductive, both in group tasks and in individual work, but guided discovery can be very successful. In this format, students generate data and respond to direct questions. If you have a particular objective, explicitly pointing students in the right direction will make them more likely to reach it. This does not necessarily make the exercise easy; it just makes it more likely to be productive.

- One way to approach proofs is to have groups engage in concrete activities, generate conjectures, and then prove or disprove conjectures. Large tasks should be subdivided into more manageable sub-tasks. For lower level courses, the task of constructing appropriate justifications, rather than formal proofs, can also be approached in this way.

- Have students make predictions and then investigate these predictions. For example, if a problem involves calculating a probability, you might have students estimate it before calculating it.

• Find a way to pre-test your activities. By offering extra credit, you might be able to entice a few students to try out the exercise before you use it in class. Another possibility is to ask a different group to meet with you each week to pilot-test your activities. This works best if the class has several groups, working together for the entire course. The benefits of this approach include getting a bird's-eye view of the dynamics of each group; another benefit is that it demonstrates to your students that you care about your teaching and that your activities are carefully planned.

• Consider developing activities for only one course at a time or part of one course at a time. One should pick opportunities carefully; it is not necessary to reform an entire course at once. This principle of progressive refinement allows for further development over time. Success in this process depends on keeping track of what you did, how it went, and how you might improve it in the future.

A Few Hints for Successful Workshop Presentations

Practice what you preach—that is, don't preach!

Storytelling can be helpful in raising and discussing issues: the leader and experienced participants can illustrate principles by relating their experiences.

Include activities for participants to reflect on what they are learning and how to apply it in their own classroom.

Give handouts that will help participants recall, implement, and extend what they learned in the workshop. Good choices of handouts include lists of guidelines for students, principles for designing activities, and selected references.

Move from the simplest procedures and activities to the more complex. This is valid advice on many levels:

• For students: Move from narrowly focused questions to open-ended questions or from simple cooperative learning techniques to more complex techniques.

• For teachers: Work from simple implementations to the more complex according to the growth in one's skill in designing and managing activities.

• For leaders: Begin with the basic workshop and work toward the more complex workshop.

Appendix

The CLUME Survey:
Responses and Summaries of Comments

Bernadette M. Baker and Nancy L. Hagelgans

Introduction

The CLUME Survey consists of questions related to the practice of cooperative learning in undergraduate mathematics courses. Many survey questions have a multiple choice part as well as opportunity for additional comments.

Invitations to take the CLUME Survey reached about 846 mathematics instructors in the spring of 1997. About 94 of these instructors answered questions in the survey, and about 20 others wrote that they were not using cooperative learning. Some respondents did not complete the entire questionnaire, and some did not explicitly follow the directions for certain questions. This appendix consists of a tally of the respondents' choices as well as summaries of their comments for each question. The counts of responses made in answering each question include all the responses, even those that appeared on partially completed questionnaires.

Question 1. In which courses have you used cooperative learning?

Responses

College Algebra	34
Precalculus	33
Calculus 1	56
Calculus II	47
Calculus III	23
Discrete Mathematics	17
Linear Algebra	14
Abstract Algebra	20
Math for Liberal Arts (Gen. Ed.)	23
Calculus for Business	19
Math for Elem. Ed. Majors	32
Math Methods for prospective teachers	15
Probability and/or Statistics	27
Differential Equations	6
Computer Programming and/or Literacy	13
Capstone course for Math majors	5

Other

Geometry	3
Mathematical Modeling	2
Developmental Math	4
Freshman Seminar	2
Elementary and Intermediate Algebra	3
AP Calculus	1
Business Math	1
Physics for Engineers	1
Advanced Calculus	1
Numerical Analysis	2
Intro. to Research	1
History of Mathematics	1
Foundations of Mathematics	1
Educational Statistics	1
Graduate Math Review Course for Secondary Math Teachers	1

Question 2. What type of activity have you used to promote a climate for cooperative learning?

Responses

Student pairs interview each other and then introduce each other to the class	25
Short presentation (each student briefly introduces him/herself to the class)	15
A regular math assignment done in groups	82
A non-math group activity (such as those involving circles and line-ups)	20

Other (*please specify*)

Group quizzes	3
Computer projects	2
Background survey	1
Discussion of homework assignments	1
Class work and tests or quizzes in groups	1
Experiments with Probability	1

Summary of Comments

Respondents to the CLUME Survey indicate that a climate for cooperative learning is fostered in different ways for different student populations. In fact, in small colleges where the students know each other and have experienced cooperative learning in other mathematics classes, little climate building is needed. On the other hand, careful development of an acceptance of cooperative learning is invaluable in many situations. Students who are comfortable with mathematics can be introduced to cooperative learning through mathematics problems that temporary groups solve. Some instructors find that initial mathematical activities are more natural, and such activities don't take time from the mathematical content of the course. A class of students who are fearful of mathematics reacts favorably to a non-threatening group activity not requiring them to do any mathematics. These students learn that they are not the only ones with math anxiety, and they begin to interact well in activities where there is no chance of failure. All students, especially commuters, benefit from activities that introduce them to each other. Climate building extends for a long period with temporary groups at some commuter colleges with high attrition rates, frequent absences, or students from a wide geographic area. Several respondents comment that students with at least some choice in members of their permanent groups seem to have a better attitude toward cooperative learning than students in the groups formed with no consideration of their preferences.

Question 3. What size groups have you used most commonly?

Responses

Group size chosen	Number of responses
2	3
2, 3	6
2, 3, 4	10
2, 3, 5	1
2, 3, 4, 5	2
2, 4	5
3	15
3, 4	18
3, 4, 5	2
3, 5	1
4	25
4, 5	1
5	2

Totals	
5 students	9
4 students	63
3 students	55
2 students	27
Other	0

Question 4. What size group do you think works best?

Responses

1 student	1
2 students	16
3 students	41
4 students	39
5 students	2
Undecided	4

Summary of Comments

Respondents to the CLUME Survey give many reasons for arranging groups of a particular size and for avoiding other sizes.

A pair of students may not be able to generate enough ideas, complete challenging assignments, or find all errors. Absenteeism is a problem when there are only two students in a group. One student may dominate a pair, and true group dynamics may not develop. On the other hand, there is relatively little disagreement, students usually can find time to meet when they have only two schedules to consider, and both students must get involved. Student pairs may generate more questions in a laboratory session than an instructor can handle alone, but a pair of students can readily see a shared computer monitor. One respondent uses groups of two only for routine exercises.

A group of five students may be too large for all students to participate in discussions, and students may have difficulty hearing each other. Too many alternative suggestions may be generated in a large group. Students may not be able to schedule meetings outside class when all group members can attend. A lazy student finds avoidance of his share of the work relatively easy in a large group. Groups of five may separate into subgroups, or four members may ignore one student. Some instructors teaching classes with an expected high attrition rate form groups of five students to avoid frequently rearranging groups when students drop the course.

The respondents generally favored groups of three or four students, and many classes contain groups of both these sizes. These groups may subdivide the work so that in a group of three a pair and a single student work separately, and in a group of four two pairs work independently. There usually is sufficient variety of experience in a group of at least three students, but when one student is absent or drops the course, the group becomes only a pair. All students in these groups can participate in the discussions, and usually they must do their part in order to complete the harder assignments.

Question 5. How were groups formed?

Responses

Students formed their own groups   39

I, the instructor, assigned students to groups   35

Combination of the two   22

Other   5

Summary of Comments

The comments written by the survey respondents indicate that many of them have tried different methods of group formation, and they continue to use different methods in different classes. For example, one instructor assigns students to groups in calculus classes but lets upper level students form their own groups. Many instructors combine the two methods by letting the students make requests and then assigning groups with an effort to honor these requests. The formation of groups is a crucial step in achieving effective cooperative learning for stable groups, but several instructors allow students to change groups, and others reorganize groups several times during a course.

Several problems emerge when students form their own groups. The groups may be too homogeneous so that the most talented students are grouped together while other groups are so weak that they are unable to handle the work. Also, students who choose their own groups may have many social conversations during class or meetings scheduled to complete assignments. However, the instructor avoids the extra work and responsibility of forming groups when the students form their own groups. Students may assess their own abilities and modes of working before forming groups or before making requests in an effort to participate in a heterogeneous group. Groups chosen by the students usually get along well and quickly become an effective team.

The main consideration in the formation of groups is the availability of common meeting times for any assignments to be completed outside class. Another important consideration is the mathematical level of the students since a group with extremely different levels usually does not function well. Some instructors who assign groups use a questionnaire to learn about the students' backgrounds and schedules, some use the interactions that they observe among students early in the course, and others assign students to groups randomly. Instructors who find several lazy freeloaders in a course may assign them to one group.

Question 6. If you assigned students to groups, what criteria did you use?

Responses

Common free time for group meetings	28
Previous mathematics courses	25
Gender	24
Some random process	24
Other particular knowledge (computer, calculator)	16
Placement test at entry	10
Average grades in previous mathematics courses	7
Age	4
Math SAT or ACT	3
Verbal SAT or ACT	1
Race	1
Average grades in all previous courses	0

Other

Residence	4
Performance in exams, previous work in course	2
Student preference	2
Personality	2
Major and/or minor	2
My assessment of ability	1
Proximity in class	1
Student's self-assessment	1
Student goals	1
Preferred learning style	1
Attitude	1

Summary of Comments

The respondents use a variety of criteria to assign students to groups, and no instructor claims with certainty that one set of criteria works well in all situations. Some of the respondents answered this question earlier. (See the summary of comments for question 5.) Again, there is general agreement that available common meeting time outside class is the most important factor. Several instructors mention that they do not form a group with only one female, unless she requests such a group, and others do not form a group of four with only one male. Most instructors strive for groups with diverse skills, and if computer work is a major part of the course, the instructors make sure that each group has at least one member with computer skills, or at least one member without computer phobia.

Question 7. How did you set the criteria?

Responses

For heterogeneous grouping (except common times for group meetings)	37
For homogeneous grouping with respect to all criteria	11
Other	9

Summary of Comments

There are far fewer comments on this question since many respondents commented on this question earlier. (See the summaries of comments for questions 5 and 6.) One instructor uses heterogeneous grouping for gender, race, and grades in the present course but does not allow only one female in a group. Another uses homogeneous grouping for place of residence and gender but otherwise heterogeneous groups. One instructor prefers homogeneous grouping with respect to calculator.

Question 8. How long are groups usually maintained?

Responses

For about a whole semester	46
For about half a semester	15
Less than half a semester	14
For a major project	15
For about a whole quarter	10
For about two semesters	2
For about half a quarter	3
Other	7

Summary of Comments

Respondents comment on their reasons for maintaining groups for a certain length of time. The goal of forming groups for a semester is to give the students time to bond and to learn to work with a team. Many instructors are flexible in reorganizing any of these stable groups that are not functioning well, and they adjust the groups to accommodate withdrawals. Other instructors think that changing groups more frequently, for each project or even every day, gives students valuable experience working with different people and different group dynamics. Some instructors use different lengths in different classes. For example, one instructor forms stable groups for the semester in calculus classes but reconfigures groups several times in courses for pre-service teachers.

Question 9. For which activities have you used cooperative learning?

Responses

Problem solving in class with class discussion immediately following	78
Homework assignments	66
Working during supervised computer labs	53
Problem solving in class on longer, harder problems or investigations	63
Projects	59
Quizzes, tests or, exams	43
Working during supervised mathematics lab period	32

Other

Writing up lab results

Problem sets covering several sections of the text

Preparing a presentation of a particular topic to the class

Group presentations of concepts and problems to the rest of the class.

Evening study rooms for homework, whoever shows up.

Summary of Comments

Respondents comment that generally in-class problem solving in groups works well. Some observe that new problems are better than homework problems since some students will not have worked on the homework problems. One instructor gives each group a different problem, and the groups present their solutions to the class. Another instructor gives relatively easy problems in class so that groups that work quickly do not have to wait for slower groups to finish the problems. The instructor learns what the students know and understand during the in-class problem-solving sessions.

Cooperative learning is very natural in the computer labs, and working in small groups helps students to overcome any anxiety related to computers. Student groups seem to be able to answer many of their questions themselves, and they depend on the instructor for help with the most difficult questions.

Homework and projects that are to be done outside class present problems with schedule conflicts. One instructor at a commuter college found that students could meet near the class time, such as the 40 minutes just prior to class. Some instructors find that difficult problems tend to promote participation by the entire group, and that the strongest members of the group readily solve easy problems alone. One instructor comments that optional evening study rooms work well when enough students come so that good discussions occur.

Respondents comment on group tests and exams. The group test questions can be harder than those for individual tests, but one instructor gives tests that require much more time than individual tests. Some instructors give group take-home exams. Several instructors write that the group tests are learning experiences. Group tests reduce test anxiety, and students prefer group tests. Several respondents express concern with individual accountability and employ methods to use group tests as only part of the grade. These methods include the following:

- give only one group test in the course,
- have groups redo a test after individuals have submitted their own work on the test,
- repeat some group quiz questions on individual tests,
- give a group take-home part of a test, and
- have groups redo the individual in-class part of the test.

Question 10. If you use cooperative learning in a structured way, mark all the strategies that you used in the classroom.

Responses

Group Problem Solving	64
Think-Pair-Share	19
Pairs-Check	15
Cooperative Review	13
Jigsaw	17

Numbered-Heads Reporting	14
Roundtable	2
Reading to Answer Questions	1

Summary of Comments

Respondents comment that they use various methods occasionally in different classes. Several instructors mention that they plan to try the various methods for the first time or that they want to improve their implementation of a certain method after trying it only a few times. One person reports that Jigsaw requires much class time.

Question 11. How do you select the cooperative learning activities?

Responses

I designed the activities.	70
I use activities from the textbook.	59
I use activities designed and tested by other colleagues.	33

Summary of Comments

Many respondents comment that they use a variety of sources to find ideas for group activities, and that they frequently adapt these activities for cooperative learning. They stress that designing successful group activities is crucial to the process of cooperative learning but that designing these activities is extremely difficult and time-consuming. One respondent suggests that there is a need for further study on why certain types of activities work well with cooperative learning groups. Others mention successful use of different types of group assignments: writing lab reports, solving challenging homework problems, writing detailed explanations of difficult reading, and reworking problems from individual tests.

Several instructors have advice about group activities:

- the problems for groups should be too difficult for one student to solve readily,
- group activities that are too difficult fail,
- a group activity should be based on a concept to be learned,
- a group activity should promote participation of all group members and interaction among the members,
- directions for the activity must be very explicit,
- open-ended and exploratory problems, problems with multiple solutions, and problems that can be solved with different methods work well as group activities, and
- students should be required to write detailed explanations of their group work.

Question 12. If you used group testing, please answer the following:

- I usually give __ group quizzes out of a total of __ quizzes during the semester/quarter.
- Do quizzes have both a group portion and an individual portion?
- I usually give __ group tests out of a total of tests during the semester/quarter.
- Do tests have both a group portion and an individual portion?
- Have you ever given a group final examination?

Responses

Sixty respondents report using group testing. Unfortunately it is impossible to interpret any numbers entered in the Web version of the questionnaire.

Summary of Comments

Respondents' comments indicate that there is a great variety in the amount of group testing in mathematics classes. Many instructors vary the number of group quizzes and tests in different classes, and others give no group tests or quizzes. Those who test students in groups also test individuals, either in part of each quiz or test, or in separate tests.

Instructors describe different types of group tests and different ways of counting grades:

- a test comprised of individual and group parts with different questions on the parts,
- a group test followed by an individual test with some questions repeated,
- an individual test followed by group work on the same problems for additional credit,
- an individual test in class with a group

take-home part,
- an individual test with the assignment of the average group grade to each student,
- a group discussion of quiz questions with no writing followed by individual work on the quiz,
- a first part of the class period for group work, but individuals write their own solutions,
- a group quiz only for bonus points to improve grades, and
- a group true/false quiz for promotion of class discussion and not for grades on the quiz.

Several instructors make observations related to the students in their own classes:
- students find group quizzes and tests less stressful than individual quizzes and tests,
- most students like the group tests,
- students share their thoughts and learn mathematics during a group test,
- students think that they have a chance at a better grade on a group test,
- some better students prefer individual tests, and
- a student may not listen to other group members.

Question 13. If you used group testing, what percentage of the total test and examination grade was earned through group tests?

Responses

10% or less	9
11–20%	13
21–30%	9
31–40%	6
41–50%	5
61–70%	1
It varies	13

Summary of Comments

Respondents offer only a few comments on this question. Most of these comments mention percentages in specific courses. One instructor alleviates students' worries by counting group work less when a student's average grade in individual work is significantly higher than the average grade in group work.

Question 14. What percentage of a student's course grade is earned through group activities?

Responses

10% or less	20
11–20%	37
21–30%	28
31–40%	12
41–50%	10
51–60%	3
61–70%	2
It varies	5

Summary of Comments

Respondents describe the ways that they vary the percentage in different classes. Several instructors who use cooperative learning in all their classes mention that they count group work more heavily in upper level courses than in lower level classes. Others state that they vary the percentage to reflect the amount of group work done for a particular class. One instructor uses grade contracts, and thus students in the same class earn different percentages of their grade through group work. Another instructor doesn't assign grades for any group work but does adjust a student's grade upward for good group participation and work.

Question 15. Do you give students instruction in cooperative learning?

Responses

Initially	47
Throughout the semester/quarter	33
No	6

Summary of Comments

Respondents who give instruction initially report that they hold an extended discussion about group attributes with the class, make a few remarks, hand out information on groups, or ask questions on group work to be answered in the students' journals. Several instructors observe that instruction on cooperative learning is more effective if it is given after the students have some experience either with informal groups or with their assigned groups. Others state that throughout the semester they regularly remind their classes of good group practices. In particular, some instructors find that instruction given to individual students or groups is very valuable when it is given as a response to observed behavior. Some instructors hold regular meetings with each group in order to discuss the group's dynamics. One instructor has students from prior classes come to talk to the current classes about cooperative learning. Some respondents mention that the goals (learning mathematics and learning to work in a team) should be emphasized along with any instruction on group behavior.

Question 16. If you use a formal set of instructions, please send a copy if you are willing to share it.

Summary of Comments

No one sent a copy of instructions. One respondent mentions having a set of ten rules that includes ways to give an opinion, to disagree with a colleague's opinion, and to resolve problems such as dominance in the group. One instructor comments that some students have difficulty working effectively in a group despite guidelines, and he attributes these difficulties to generally poor social skills. Another instructor comments that, although students know what constitutes good group behavior, some students do not apply this knowledge to their own group activities.

Question 17. How do you monitor groups?

Responses

Informal observations	77
Formal meetings	32
Questionnaires	22
Student journals	21

Other
Short reports
email
Progress reports
Daily class participation forms

Project presentation and group ratings
Group reports

Summary of Comments

Respondents report that they use multiple methods for monitoring the groups, but informal observations usually are included among these methods. Instructors find informal observations valuable in classes where the group activities take place during the class or scheduled lab times. These observations are especially effective in smaller classes where the instructor can walk around the room and converse with each group while all the groups are working on a group activity.

Formal meetings with each student group work well for some instructors. These conferences may be scheduled for all groups one or more times throughout the course, or they may be arranged only in response to difficulties within a group. One problem with this monitoring technique is that some groups cannot find a time when all members can meet with the instructor outside class time.

Instructors whose students keep journals generally find that this is an effective method for learning about the groups' activities and any developing problems within the groups. One respondent reports that email journals and responses are easier to handle than paper journals. On the other hand, one instructor's students think that journals involve too much extra work, and the instructor now uses other methods to monitor groups.

Several respondents express concern about the honesty of the students in reporting their groups' dynamics. Students seem reluctant to fully describe any difficulties within their groups either in writing or speaking to their instructors.

Question 18. What nonproductive behavior did you encounter with your groups?

Responses

One or more students did not contribute to discussions	61
Students divided work and then had little interaction	46
One or more students dominated discussions	45

Students could not find a common time to meet	52
Some students did not attend group meetings	56
Students did not want to meet outside of class	44
There were excessive absences of one or more students	41
Group split into sub-groups that had little interaction	23
One or more students did not do a fair share of the work	22

Other
One group member did all the work
Students would socialize

Summary of Comments

There are very few comments. One respondent writes that during seven years of cooperative learning all these problems had occurred but that there is not much difficulty in any one semester.

Question 19. Please describe the problems of any dysfunctional groups or individuals.

Summary of Comments

Several respondents write that they have encountered most or all of the behaviors listed in the previous question at one time or another. They stress that these difficulties do not occur frequently.

Individual shortcomings and students' personality conflicts cause many problems within groups. An occasional student refuses to work with a group under any conditions. Other students expend little effort on the course, including the group activities. Groups may ostracize any members who do not do their part, come late or unprepared to meetings, do not attend group meetings and conferences, or dominate unfairly. One respondent describes an older student who tried to demand that her group spend inordinate amounts of time checking over the homework.

Group formation practices cause some problems. A group with exceptionally weak students who cannot do the work at all becomes discouraged.

A less advanced student in a group of strong students becomes intimidated, and the abler students become annoyed with the questions asked. Even though group members initially have schedules compatible with group meetings, changes in sports and jobs may mean that a group finds it difficult to meet outside class as the course progresses.

Question 20. What did you try in attempting to handle any problems with cooperative learning?

Responses

I met with the members of any such group individually	49
I re-formed the groups	39
I met with any such groups as a whole	42
I allowed the students to re-form groups	33
I wrote suggestions in student journals	10
I usually ignored the problems	12

Other
I encourage appropriate behavior
I discuss problems as they occur with the group

Summary of Comments

Many respondents use a variety of methods in addressing problems within groups and choose methods that will be effective in specific situations. Some instructors re-form groups, but then new groups must get acquainted, and some students do not want to move to new groups. Infrequently, the newly formed groups may include one disruptive student who has great difficulty working with other students.

Communication with individuals and groups in the classroom or the office, in student journals, or through email is the first method many instructors try whenever a group problem is observed. One instructor writes that, when addressing serious problems, he first works with the individuals in the group before holding a group conference. Several instructors mention that they assume the role of a mediator who states options and then lets the students solve their own problems within the group. Only one instructor mentions decreasing the frequency of the group assignments. Another provides a procedure that a group can use to "fire" a member.

Question 21. When you communicate with students about their problems with cooperative learning, what is your usual point of view?

Responses

I present options and then let the students solve the problems	46
I make specific suggestions in an effort to improve the functioning of the group	38
It's up to the students to work out their own problems	27

Summary of Comments

Respondents generally have the attitude that students should solve their own problems. Instructors become involved by making suggestions only when the students seem unable to work out their own difficulties. As a last resort, instructors give specific directions rather than presenting options.

Question 22. Do you expect students to work together in groups outside of class? If so, how have you structured this, especially for commuter students?

Responses

Yes (with qualifying comments)	48
No (with qualifying comments)	23

Summary of Comments

Respondents who expect groups to work together outside class consider the students' schedules and residences when forming the groups at the beginning of the course. Instructors mention the following methods that help the groups to work on projects outside class:

- have projects due at least a week after assigned,
- adjust due dates of projects to fit times that students can meet,
- have groups submit a schedule of times when they can hold regular group meetings,
- let students start projects during class time,
- provide a room where students can meet immediately before and after class, and
- encourage the students to communicate via telephone (even conference calls) and email.

Question 23. Was technology used by groups in your class? If so, circle all that apply.

Responses

Graphing calculators	62
Computer algebra system	41
Mathematical programming language	27
Graphing calculators with symbolic capability	14
Software accompanying a textbook	6
Special software	
Minitab	7
Geometer's Sketchpad	6
Netscape	2

Other technology include a graphing program interfaced through a web browser, spreadsheets, a 3-D plotting program, MPP, Gyrographics, LaTeX, TI GraphLink, Eudora, JMP statistical package, Compustat, FORTRAN, Pascal, LOGO, Visual BASIC, Microsoft Office, Excel, Word, MATLAB, ESG, and StatsView

Question 24. What was the effect of the use of technology on the groups?

Responses

Improved group dynamics	37
Different effects on different groups	27
No obvious effect	22

Summary of Comments

Respondents who think that the use of technology improves group dynamics find that students are able to talk more readily about the computer results than about the mathematics at first. The shared use of a computer forces students to concentrate on the same aspect of a problem, and they discuss what appears on the computer screen. In some cases, a student who is relatively weak in mathematics gains the respect of group members by contributing expertise with the computer or the software. In fact, several instructors mention that in some groups an attitude develops that the group is a team against a common enemy, the computer. Students help each other overcome any difficulties with the computer software or the graphing calculator. One instructor's students are anxious to show each other new tricks with Geometer's Sketchpad, and students of another respondent like to discuss the various ways to use their graphing calculators. Productive discussions result when students are trying to explain how the computer or calculator obtains results.

One respondent notes that any group in which students own different calculators struggles over new techniques more than groups whose members own calculators that are all alike. One instructor finds that time spent on introduction of certain software detracts from the course and the group process. Another instructor observes that a student with previous computer experience may initially dominate the group. Occasionally one student's aversion to all technology affects the attitude of the whole group. One instructor finds that use of a graphing calculator has little effect on interaction among students in a group.

Question 25. How would you describe your teaching experience using cooperative learning?

Responses

Generally successful	52
Some problems, but some positive student gains	42
Generally too problematic to continue using cooperative learning	4

Question 26. During group activities, my role as an instructor is best described by:

Responses

I usually make suggestions on ways to attack the problem(s), but stay out of the process.	57
I try to turn all questions back to the group and rarely give hints on problems.	30
I temporarily become a member of the group.	15
Other	2

Summary of Comments

Respondents change their roles to accommodate different situations. Even when they want to encourage investigation and group independence, they answer some questions. Rather than actually doing the problems, instructors help groups by making suggestions on how to start a problem. Instructors give more help when students must produce results in a given time, such as during one laboratory or class period. Some respondents think that students should be allowed to struggle and to make mistakes and that the students rather than the instructor should verify the results of group work.

Question 27. How is the attrition rate affected by cooperative learning?

Responses

Cooperative learning seems to have no effect on attrition rates.	41
Fewer students drop courses in which cooperative learning is a major feature.	29
Depends on the level of the course.	4
More students drop such a course.	2

Summary of Comments

Several instructors comment that the use of cooperative learning provides more social support for students and a sense of security in courses that they find difficult. Another reports that students develop a sense of loyalty to their group although this instructor uses cooperative learning in courses where little or no attrition is expected. Two instructors using C4L report a substantial number of students drop in the beginning of the course, although it is not clear if this is due to cooperative learning, fear of computers, or other factors.

Question 28. How did most students react to cooperative learning?

Responses

Very positively	16
Positively	63
Neutral	15
Negatively	5

Summary of Comments

The positive comments indicate that many students enjoy working in their groups, like getting to know more classmates, and generally perceive that cooperative learning improves their learning and their grade. In-class group work is more positively received than group work required outside of class. One instructor writes that students always want to work with their friends, but that they are more honest in assessing others' performances when they are working with strangers. Another respondent comments that students appreciate being able to express their confusion and ask questions of their peers rather than asking the teacher in front of the whole class. One instructor observes that students believe that sometimes a peer explains the concept better than the teacher does.

One instructor reports that upper division students like being able to see how their peers think about doing problems. Another states that cooperative learning has a beneficial effect on students' attitudes. Several respondents find that students believe cooperative learning improves their grade while others think it has little or no effect on their grade.

One faculty member reports much better acceptance of cooperative learning when she starts a 90-minute class with a 10-minute mini-lecture and introduction to the topic followed by the group activities. Several respondents comment that students who have not experienced cooperative learning earlier often need some time to get used to it

and accept it (and often like it by the end of the term). Another instructor states that the students know that cooperative learning is required in his or her courses along with lots of writing in complete sentences and finds that students are thankful for the help they receive from their group.

Another instructor reports that she has more success in using cooperative learning in algebra than in teacher education courses, while two other faculty members report the opposite experience: more success in teacher education courses. One respondent reports better acceptance of cooperative learning in computer science classes than in calculus classes. Engineering students also are reported to be more reluctant to using cooperative learning than mathematics, pre-medical, or non-education majors.

Negative comments indicate student dissatisfaction with being required to work with other students, especially by brighter, more introverted students, and by non-teacher education majors. Some students complain that cooperative learning courses require more work than lecture courses, complain about poor attendance of their group members, or express the belief that the only real benefit is being able to split the required work into four parts. Several faculty members report that students will tolerate whatever one requires of them, but they may not like it; however, in these instructors' opinions, no one is harmed by the use of cooperative learning.

Question 29. How would you describe the effect of cooperative learning in the course syllabi?

Responses

The usual number of topics was covered	45
Fewer topics were covered	36
More topics were covered	5

Summary of Comments

Of those who cover fewer topics, many say they prioritize to cover the most important topics while others report that they make students responsible for more material that is not discussed in class. Some respondents say they use a mix of cooperative learning and traditional lectures to minimize the effect on the number of topics covered.

Some instructors who cover fewer topics indicate that the topics that are discussed are done so in more depth than previously and that students display deeper understanding of the topics that are covered. Some instructors use cooperative learning group activities only for "outside of class time" projects to minimize the effect on the syllabus topics.

If the course is a terminal one (not a prerequisite for other courses), then the number of topics covered is less important. If many instructors in an institution use cooperative learning, the first course progresses more slowly as students adjust to group work, but in subsequent courses, the pace is more similar to non-cooperative learning courses. One instructor tried having different groups master different assigned topics and present to other groups, but reports mixed results.

One instructor assigns fewer homework problems when using cooperative learning; another reports proving fewer theorems but covers the spirit, if not the letter, of the syllabus. Several instructors express frustration with the amount of time needed for students' understanding to develop.

Question 30. What gains have you observed in your students' approach to learning mathematics, attitudes toward mathematics, or skills and understanding of mathematics while using cooperative learning?

Summary of Comments

Students are more reflective, spend more time on task, are more willing to try to figure things out, and more self-confident about their ability to do mathematics. Students become better thinkers and listeners and are more willing to conjecture. They are less passive, less math anxious, more independent in exploring, less intimidated by mistakes, more open to learning mathematics, and more willing to attempt unusual problems in groups. They can verbalize their thinking and learning. Students exhibit more conceptual learning.

Over time, students' attitudes towards mathematics improve and their views of what mathematics is changes. Students gain confidence in their ability to do mathematics, and struggling

students get support to persevere from other members of the group. Students learn that different people have different strengths, and they learn to use each other as sounding boards and resources. Group work humanizes mathematics for students. In mathematics education courses, students become less fearful of mathematics and the prospect of having to teach mathematics.

Students are better able to use the language of mathematics. They gain the experience of working on real-world problems requiring oral presentations and written reports. In a proof oriented course, students become more comfortable with abstract thought. Improved problem-solving skill results from exposure to more strategies of others in the group. Students are more willing to discuss attempts, and they exhibit less "all or nothing" behavior about problems. Group members discuss mathematics more, learn to ask more questions, and work more regularly on problems throughout the course.

The peer teaching in a group improves comprehension and confidence. Students learn to use their intuition and common sense in solving problems. They also learn that not all problems have simple solutions and that some problems are not solvable. Students come to the realization that they need to remember the mathematics learned in prerequisite courses, and that they may have to look outside the text or lectures for information needed to solve problems.

Good students can get stronger by taking on leadership roles, while weaker students may become weaker or may strengthen their understanding, depending on the functioning of the group. It helps stronger students to have the occasion to try to explain ideas to weaker students and it may help weaker students to see stronger students in action. Some students end up taking additional courses in mathematics that they had not planned on because of their positive experience using cooperative learning.

Students become more critical of their thinking processes and others' thinking processes as well as the correctness of solutions. The meaning of proof changes as students think about convincing others in the group that something is true (or false). They have a better concept of what an assumption is and what is a logical conclusion of their investigation. Because of the use of technology, some instructors believe that students are somewhat less able with manipulations of, for example, derivatives, but have a better understanding of what a derivative is and how it is applied.

Some instructors caution that since the content, pedagogy, and, in some cases, the use of technology all change, it is difficult to separate out what effects can be attributed to cooperative learning. Others observe improvement in some, but not all students. Some respondents believe gains depend on the particular class. Some instructors believe that fragile students benefit the most while better students are not always as positive about their group experiences.

Upper division mathematics majors appreciate the opportunity to discuss mathematics with other interested students. They sometimes form groups that continue to work together in subsequent semesters, especially in other mathematics classes.

Question 31. What gains have you observed in your students' social behavior while using cooperative learning?

Summary of Comments

Students become more vocal and more able to ask questions about what they need to know. Shy students tend to become more confident and over confident students tend to become more helpful. They learn to work better with others, develop skill in organizing themselves, and learn to communicate clearly with each other. Students develop skills in presentation and articulation of mathematics. The classroom is no longer a competitive environment and there is an increase in civility and courtesy. There is better class attendance since the students feel a sense of responsibility to the group.

Esprit de corps develops in cooperative learning classes. Some respondents report that the class takes on more of a family atmosphere, the students make new friends, and they are more talkative. They are supportive of each other and strive to be sure everyone in the group understands. The classroom is a livelier place, and there is a buzz in the room. Students are more likely to interact outside of class with a wider range of students.

Students develop a stronger relationship with their peers and become interested in each other's learning. Students become more tolerant of individual differences, other viewpoints and

personalities when they see that everyone has something to contribute. Working in groups can be a consciousness expanding experience, especially for those in groups with members who have personal difficulties such as single parenthood, disabilities, or full-time jobs. They learn they are not alone in struggling to learn a topic, and this realization increases confidence.

One faculty member suggests that because cooperative learning helps the loners or shy students become part of the community, it may help retention in keeping some students from dropping out of the class or of college. Another reports four marriages have emerged from groups. One instructor notices that students may shift roles, for example, from class clown to motivator. Finally, some respondents report that they notice no change in their students' social behavior.

Question 32. Describe any negative approaches to learning mathematics, negative attitudes toward mathematics, negative social behaviors, or decline in skill or understanding of mathematics that you have observed while using cooperative learning.

Summary of Comments

Several comments involve lazy students. Some students react negatively to the fact that they can no longer fake it, and others like cooperative learning because they can wait for someone else in the group to do the thinking and the work. Freeloaders can hang on a little longer before they drop. Individual members of a group do not always take the responsibility of individual learning thus reducing their skill and understanding of mathematics. They depend too much on the group for finding the answers. Students who want to avoid studying and simply imitate examples are usually frustrated in cooperative learning classes.

To an extent cooperative learning legitimizes cheating by permitting a person who has done little to receive the same credit as the person who has learned much. When a strong student carries a group, it encourages other students to rely on that person to do the work. The flip side occurs when the stronger student takes on the toughest job, but fails to communicate to the others what she is doing, or how. Some students use group work as a way to avoid actually doing mathematics. Some are even able to seem very productive within their group while doing this, by taking charge of such things as setting up group meetings, organizing and collating assignments, *etc*. Some students think that they learn the subject best by doing their own work, and they focus on what they are assigned to do. Sometimes students do not want to help anybody and are concerned only with their own learning. They may simply refuse to work with others. The noisy classroom irritates some students.

Respondents comment on weaker students. Some weaker students like to hide in mathematics classes. Since group projects expose their weak backgrounds to their peers, they may become more aloof and unteachable. Sometimes weak students are too accepting of others' incorrect thinking. Exposure to this degree of error or inelegance may not occur in a non-cooperative environment. Weaker students may get slightly higher grades than they deserve, although their attitudes don't seem to change much. Students tend to skip classes or to have a more individualistic position in class if they don't buy into cooperative learning because it forces them to uncover their mathematics weakness or because they think they are better challenged with regular individual assignments.

Respondents write about their more talented students also. Some talented students are reluctant to participate because they believe they need to learn the material individually and not rely on others. They fear that others will drag down their performance. If talented students don't buy into helping others, they begrudge the extra time. Well-prepared students experience frustration and feel "held back" by the slower students in their group. Really good students don't get the topic coverage that they would be exposed to under a more traditional approach. They sometimes don't practice computational skills as much as they really should in order to succeed at high levels. There is concern that some budding mathematicians may be lost.

Integrating group learning, activities, projects, and computer technology can be overwhelming to students who complain that the structure is not as organized as they expect. The negative behaviors are usually related to grouping and its logistic problems and not mathematics itself. Often there is not as much rote drill so some skills are not as practiced, but general understanding is usually greater.

An organizational comment concerns the difficulty of answering everyone's questions when there are too many little groups. Unless the class is very small, students may spend too much time with their hands in the air as they wait for the instructor's help.

Dysfunctional groups are the focus of a number of comments. Shy persons may remain shy, causing inclusion concerns. Students in groups that choose (despite warnings) to split assignments rather than completing them cooperatively usually do not gain the skills or understanding that they would have had they worked individually. Some students are never able to break free of the competitive model, continue to dominate their groups, and try to do all the work without letting the rest of the group members participate (while complaining that the others never do their share). Some students simply do not attend group meetings.

Some groups resist really trying to understand, and they attempt to rely on memorization. If students fail to perform in a small group they become more readily discouraged than in a larger group. Very negative students can feed on each other and increase the negativity in the group. One respondent reports having about one student per semester who is violently opposed to group work and cooperative learning; in this instructor's experience, the problem occurs most frequently with an older student returning to school for teacher certification.

Criticism of the cooperative learning teaching style comes from both students and colleagues. From students, negative attitudes are of the "you're supposed to teach me" or "the instructor does not do his job" or "the group explains better than the instructor" variety. Colleagues also may feel that someone who uses cooperative learning is not teaching. Sometimes the teacher allows students to be uncomfortable for a long period of time because there is learning going on. The student may learn but leave the class with some bitterness. Some students really prefer the lecture method; other students will become obstinate if they can't understand a problem and refuse to engage themselves.

Some respondents report no negative behavior or attitudes.

Question 33. If your students assessed their work within the group and/or the way the group interacts, please answer the following:

- How was the assessment made? Please describe here (or send copies of) any assessment materials you used that you are willing to share.
- Did you include any self-assessment of group work within the grading structure? _____ If so, how?

Responses

No	17
Yes	2

Summary of Comments

Many respondents use peer and self-assessments outside of the grading structure. A number of instructors employ written reflections, journals, questionnaires, or Likert scale instruments for students to comment on group functioning and their own behavior in their group. Some do this once or twice per semester while others use self and group assessment as part of each group assignment. Some instructors respond through journal feedback to such analyses. Although not part of the recorded grade, one instructor reports having group members grade themselves and each other on each project, while another requires a "grade" for each participant agreed upon by the group as part of the materials handed in on each project. One instructor has students assess the relative value of various types of group activity used within the class; group re-do exams and in-class discussion are rated highly.

Some instructors object to the idea of having students grade each other's participation, and they do not use this method. Others report trying this type of assessment but being dissatisfied with it and abandoning it.

Most respondents indicate they do not use self-assessment of group work within the grading structure. Of those who do, one instructor assigns 10% of a project grade to peer/self assessment; another assigns a certain number of total points to the graded project and allows the group to assign the number of points to individual members based on their contributions. Two possible biases in this method are pointed out: weaker students who ask more questions may assign fewer points to themselves and a stronger student may monopolize the conversation and the group work in order to get more points for himself. These problems with self-assessment caused one instructor to abandon its use.

Another instructor who incorporates assessments in grading allows the group to not list any member who did not contribute substantially to the project. The instructor then works with the offending member and the group to ensure this does not happen in the future. A different strategy is to have students assess oral presentations of class members and themselves using criteria provided by the instructor. The arithmetic average of these become part of the student's grade. One instructor has students write frequent reflections on their contribution to a positive learning environment within the group. The instructor responds to these writings and uses them as a basis for the participation grade for the class.

Three instructors share some of the items on their assessment form for group work. The items on one open-response form include:

- Has it been helpful to work with a classmate? If so, what are the benefits?
- Have there been problems working together? If so, specify the nature of the problems.
- Do you feel it would be more beneficial for you to work with a different teammate during the remainder of the semester?
- Add any other comments you think might be helpful.
- Another instructor adds these six additional questions to the mandatory course evaluation form. Instructions are to respond in writing, saying as much or as little as desired:
- Do your group members generally cooperate in your group?
- Do you try to listen to other's ideas and build upon them?
- Does everyone participate and no one dominates?
- Is the pace of the group about right for you? Too fast? Too slow?
- Do you like the idea of groups? Explain.
- Any complaints or suggestions about the use of groups?

The third instructor, who sent a sample of the form used by the students for assessing each member in the group, uses a Likert scale including these items:

- participates in group discussions
- is willing to explain mathematical ideas to the group
- encourages others in the group to explain their ideas to the group
- stays focused on the task at hand
- contributes his share to group projects

The average score for each student is used as a part of the course grade.

Question 34. Have you experienced conflicts on your campus caused by the difference between "traditional" instructors versus "cooperative learning" sections/courses and "cooperative learning" instructors?

Responses

No	21
Yes	11

Summary of Comments

The nature of the conflicts includes having difficulty finding a textbook acceptable to instructors in both cooperative learning sections and traditional sections of the same course and skepticism about the use of computer systems in teaching mathematics and the grading standards in cooperative learning classes. One instructor indicates she must keep quiet on campus about using cooperative learning and that this conflict is the reason for not using permanent groups. Several instructors report general animosity by longtime colleagues to any effort in teaching improvement. Reasons for negative reactions include protection of research time, fear of making changes in longtime habits, and skepticism about the efficacy of discovery learning.

One respondent indicates instructors in the client disciplines complain rather than colleagues in the mathematics department. Another reports that non-cooperative learning colleagues refuse to teach certain cooperative learning courses and so far, there have been other teaching assignments available. One instructor indicates that another instructor harasses

students in the cooperative learning course if those students subsequently enroll in sections of his courses. At one campus, tension was present during the first two quarters when cooperative learning was used, but the situation calmed after that time.

Suggestions to ease conflicts include working on other department problems as a team in order to foster more openness, trying to convert colleagues to cooperative learning, and conducting research in cooperative learning classes to show evidence of its effectiveness to colleagues. One respondent is collecting longitudinal data on the progress of C4L students through future classes in hopes of changing some opinions about cooperative learning among colleagues. Another instructor reports the main problem involves very negative peer evaluations because the evaluators are unsympathetic to the techniques of cooperative learning.

Question 35. Do you notice any difference in the course evaluation comments by students now from those you received before you began using cooperative learning? _____ If yes, please describe.

Responses

No	10
Better/More Positive Evaluations	21
Worse/More Negative Evaluations	11
Unclear answer	7

Summary of Comments

Among the comments indicating more positive evaluations when using cooperative learning, students state the group work is their "salvation" and that required courses are less boring because they are actively involved in class. Especially in upper level classes, students are enthusiastic about the *esprit de corps* that develops in the classroom. Many students like projects while others complain about them. Students also favor a more active approach to learning and are more willing to express their opinions in class, possibly because they are more confident in their learning.

Respondents include reasons for negative evaluations. Students do not like the instructor to expect exercises to be completed in a group before the instructor explains the material and presents examples. In another class, students do not want to be expected to work on group projects outside of class, and they view the instructor's behavior when using groups as "not teaching." Some students indicate that they prefer to learn from lectures, and they do not want to learn from reading on their own and from exercises within their group. Several instructors indicate that their course evaluations were lower the first semester or two that they used cooperative learning but the evaluations have improved in subsequent semesters. Another faculty member concurs in this opinion by indicating that lower evaluations depend, at least in part, on whether this is the students' first experience of group work.

In an Abstract Algebra course, perhaps students' dislike of the programming language ISETL affects their opinion of cooperative learning. Another instructor reports that students believe that the explanations in a cooperative learning class are not as good as in other sections since more of the students in the cooperative learning class attend the group study sessions organized by the cooperative learning instructor. Other instructors comment that evaluations depend to a great extent on the level of the course in which groups are used. One faculty member indicates that students perceive her as even harder and more demanding than before, but the instructor believes she is teaching less content than previously. One instructor, whose evaluations while using group work were very poor, decided to limit its use to only 10–20% of the course grade, and then evaluations improved significantly.

Among comments indicating an unclear effect of the use of cooperative learning, one instructor states that since both content and pedagogy are changing, it is difficult to attribute the change to a single factor. Cooperative learning replaces a lecture format and a reform curriculum replaces traditional content. In another instance, the instructor changed schools, from a research institution to a liberal arts college, so again, it is hard to compare the evaluations. In several instances, instructors comment that evaluations are certainly no worse when they use cooperative learning, and are perhaps somewhat better.

Question 36. Please make any other comment that you think might be helpful. We would appreciate descriptions of your experiences in particular classes and with particular groups as well as your evaluation of the effects of particular aspects of your implementation of cooperative learning.

Summary of Comments

Several comments concern time issues regarding cooperative learning: deciding how much time to allot an activity and deciding what topics to leave out so that group work can fit into the syllabus. Also, respondents mention the time required to develop cooperative learning activities, and the problem of fitting in this time commitment with heavy teaching loads and continuing research and publication expectations. Administrative support for the use of cooperative learning does not necessarily ease these time conflicts in the experience of some respondents if expectations don't also change. Frustrations in dealing with groups whose members have widely different ideas, no ideas, a lack of necessary background, or a slow work rate are also related to the time issues. Others report that students are more efficient at spreading understanding, especially if faculty refrain from giving too much prompting.

Evaluation issues are also a concern. Some instructors believe that in cooperative learning situations, some students get very lazy and let others do all the work, or that group reports allow some students to hide from real learning. Some instructors who use group work also require individual written and oral reports to keep track of individual learning. On the other hand, one faculty member comments that students work harder in groups because both the instructor's expectations are higher and their peers see what they are doing. For this reason, this instructor believes that she knows more about the progress of individual students than in courses with strictly individual evaluation.

Several respondents urge others to start slowly, introducing just an activity or two. This allows both the instructor and students to adjust to the use of group work and also keeps friction to a minimum with one's traditional colleagues. A number of the respondents report that they use cooperative learning as a part of their overall teaching strategy in conjunction with lecture in trying to meet the needs of all students. These instructors also indicate they use a mixture of group and individual assessments in their courses.

Bibliography

Introduction

Both *A Practical Guide to Cooperative Learning in Collegiate Mathematics* by Hagelgans *et al* and *Readings in Cooperative Learning for Undergraduate Mathematics* edited by Dubinsky, Mathews, and Reynolds include extensive bibliographies. This listing is a selected bibliography focusing on useful sources for post-secondary level instructors who are either beginning to use cooperative learning strategies or looking for ways to extend their use of cooperative learning.

This bibliography is organized in two sections. The first section lists books and articles about teaching and learning and includes the references cited by the authors throughout this volume. The second section is a listing of textbooks and classroom resource materials that the authors have found well suited to a cooperative learning environment at the community college or undergraduate level.

I. Selected Bibliography

Aldrich, V. H., E. W. Cohen, and L. M. Hartsell. *Collaborative Learning Manual.* Reading, MA: Addison-Wesley, 1995.

Archimedes. On the Method. In *Great Books*, Vol. 7, pp. 569–596, *Encyclopedia Britannica*.

Aronson, E., N. *et al*. *The Jigsaw Classroom.* Beverly Hills, CA: Sage Publications, 1978.

Artzt, Alice and Claire M. Newman. *How to Use Cooperative Learning in the Mathematics Class*. Reston, VA: National Council of Teachers of Mathematics, 1990.

Asiala, M. *et al*. A Framework for Research and Curriculum Development in Undergraduate Mathematics Education. In *Research in Collegiate Mathematics Education II*, edited by E. Dubinsky, J. Kaput, and A. Schoenfeld. The American Mathematical Society, (1996), pp. 1–32.

Barnes, Douglas, James Britton, and Mike Torbe. *Language, the Learner and the School* 2nd ed. Portsmouth, NH: Boynton/Cook, 1986.

Bennett, Albert and Linda Foreman. *Visual Mathematics*. Salem, OR: Math Learning Center, 1991.

Bennett, Albert, Eugene Maier, and Ted Nelson. *Math and the Mind's Eye*. Salem, OR: Math Learning Center, 1991.

Bittinger, Marvin L. A Review of Discovery, *The Mathematics Teacher*, 61 (February), 1968: 140–146.

Bonwell, Charles C. and James A. Eison. Active Learning: Creating Excitement in the Classroom. *ASHE-ERIC Higher Education Report*, No. 1. Washington, DC: The George Washington University, School of Education and Human Development, 1991.

Bosworth, K. and S. J. Hamilton (editors). *Collaborative Learning: Underlying Processes and Effective Techniques*. San Francisco: Jossey-Bass, 1994.

Britton, James. *Language and Learning*. Portsmouth, NH: Boynton/Cook, 1970.

Brody, Celeste and Neil Davidson (editors). *Professional Development for Cooperative Learning*. Albany, NY: SUNY Press, 1998.

Brubacher, Mark, Rider Payne, and Kemp Rickett. *Perspectives on Small Group Learning*. Oakvale, Ontario, Canada: Rubicon Publishing, 1990.

Bruffee, K. *Collaborative Learning: Higher Education, Interdependence, and the Authority of Knowledge*. Baltimore, MD: Johns Hopkins University Press, 1993.

Bruner, Jerome S. *The Process of Education*. Cambridge: Harvard University Press, 1960.

Bruner, Jerome S. *Toward a Theory of Instruction*. Cambridge: Belknap Press, 1966.

Bruner, Jerome S. Bruner on the Learning of Mathematics: A 'Process Orientation'. In *Readings in Secondary School Mathematics*, edited by Douglas A. Aichele and Robert E. Reys. Boston, MA: Prindle, Weber, & Schmidt, 1971, 2nd ed. 1977.

Campbell, Bill and Karl Smith. *New Paradigms for College Teaching*. Edina, MN: Interaction Book Company, 1996.

Clark, J. M. *et al. An Examination of Student Performance Data in Recent RUMEC Studies*, in preparation.

Cohen, Elizabeth. *Designing Group Work: Strategies for the Heterogeneous Classroom*. New York: Teachers College Press, Columbia University, 1986, 2nd ed. 1994.

Cole, Mildred *et al. Unifying Concepts and Processes in Elementary Mathematics, University of Maryland Mathematics Project*. Rockleigh, NJ: Allyn and Bacon, 1978.

Collison, Judith. Is Cooperation Appropriate in Testing? *Cooperative Learning*, 14 (1993): 21–22.

Cooper, James *et al. Cooperative Learning and College Instruction: Effective Use of Student Learning Teams*. Carson, CA: Center for Quality Education, 1989.

Crabill, Calvin. Small Group Learning in the Secondary Mathematics Classroom. In *Cooperative Learning in Mathematics: A Handbook for Teachers*, edited by Neil Davidson. Menlo Park: Addison-Wesley, CA, 1990.

Cross, K. Patricia and Thomas A. Angelo. *Classroom Assessment Techniques: A Handbook for Faculty*. National Center for Research to Improve Postsecondary Teaching and Learning, 1988.

Czarnocha, Bronislaw (Bronisuave). The Constructivist Teacher as a Researcher, *Educacion Matematica*, (Mexico), 11 (2), 1999: 53–63.

Davidson, Neil. The Small Group Discovery Method as Applied in Calculus Instruction. *American Mathematical Monthly*, 78 (7), 1971: 789–791.

Davidson, Neil. Small Group Learning and Teaching in Mathematics: A Selective Review of the Research. In *Learning to Cooperate, Cooperating to Learn*, edited by R. Slavin *et al.* New York: Plenum Press, 1985, pp. 211–230.

Davidson, Neil. *Cooperative Learning in Mathematics: A Handbook for Teachers*. Menlo Park, Addison-Wesley, CA: 1990.

Davidson, Neil. Cooperative and Collaborative Learning: An Integrative Perspective. In *Creativity and Collaborative Learning: A Practical Guide for Empowering Teachers and Students*, edited by J. Thousand, R. Villa, and A. Nevin. Baltimore, MD: Brookes Publishing, 1994, pp. 13–30.

Davidson, Neil and Frances Gulick. *Abstract Algebra: An Active Learning Approach*, Boston: Houghton Mifflin, 1976.

Davidson, Neil, and Frances Gulick. Instructor's Manual for Abstract Algebra: An Active Learning Approach, Houghton Miflin Company, Boston, 1976.

Davidson, Neil and Diana Lambdin Kroll. An Overview of Research on Cooperative Learning Related to Mathematics, *Journal for Research in Mathematics Education*, 22 (5), 1991: 362–365.

Davidson, Neil, Ronald McKeen, and Theodore Eisenberg. Curriculum Construction

Bibliography

with Student Input, *The Mathematics Teacher*, 66 (3), 1973: 271–275.

Davidson, Neil and Toni Worsham (editors). *Enhancing Thinking Through Cooperative Learning*. New York: Teachers College Press, 1992.

Dubinsky, Ed. On Teaching Mathematical Induction, I. *Journal of Mathematical Behavior*, 5, 1986: 305–317.

Dubinsky, Ed. A Learning Theory Approach to Calculus, In *Proceedings of the St. Olaf Conference*, Northfield, MN: St. Olaf, 1989.

Dubinsky, Ed. On Teaching Mathematical Induction, II. *Journal of Mathematical Behavior*, 8, 1989: 285–304.

Dubinsky, E. Constructive Aspects of Reflective Abstraction in Advanced Mathematical Thinking. In *Epistemological Foundations of Mathematical Experience*, edited by Leslie P. Steffe. New York: Springer-Verlag, 1991.

Dubinsky, Ed. A Learning Theory Approach to Calculus. In *Symbolic Computation in Undergraduate Mathematics Education*, edited by Z. Karian. MAA Notes, No. 24. Washington DC: The Mathematical Association of America, 1992, pp. 48–55.

Dubinsky, Ed. A Theory and Practice of Learning College Mathematics. In *Mathematical Thinking and Problem Solving*, edited by A. Schoenfeld. Hillsdale: Erlbaum, 1994, pp. 221-243.

Dubinsky, E., J. Kaput, and A. Schoenfeld. *Research in Collegiate Mathematics Education, I, II, and III*. American Mathematical Society, 1994, 1996,and 1998.

Dubinsky, Ed, David Mathews, Barbara E. Reynolds (editors). 1997. *Readings in Cooperative Learning for Undergraduate Mathematics*. MAA Notes, Number 44. Washington, D.C.: The Mathematical Association of America.

Dubinsky, Ed and M. McDonald. *Theory of Learning in Undergraduate Mathematics Education Research*, to appear.

Dubinsky, Ed and Keith E. Schwingendorf. Constructing Calculus Concepts: Cooperation in a Computer

Laboratory. In *The Laboratory Approach to Teaching Calculus*, edited by L. Carl Leinbach *et al*. Washington, DC: The Mathematical Association of America, 1991, pp. 47–70.

Finkel, D. L. and G. S. Monk. Teachers and Learning Groups: Dissolution of the Atlas Complex. In *Learning in Groups*, edited by C. Bouton and R. Y. Garth. San Francisco: Jossey-Bass, 1993, pp. 83–97.

Gabelnick, F., J. MacGregor, R. S. Matthews, and B. L. Smith. *Learning Communities: Creating Connections among Students, Faculty, and Disciplines*. San Francisco: Jossey-Bass, 1990.

Gagne, Robert. *The Conditions of Learning*. New York: Holt, Rinehart & Winston, 1965.

Goodsell, A. S., M. Moher, and V. Tinte. *Collaborative Learning: A Sourcebook for Higher Education*. University Park, PA: National Center on Postsecondary Teaching, Learning, and Assessment, 1992.

Graves, Ted. The Controversy over Group Rewards in Cooperative Classrooms, *Educational Leadership*, 48 (7), 1991: pp. 77–79.

Hadamard, Jacques. *The Psychology of Invention in the Mathematical Field*. Princeton, NJ: Princeton University Press, 1945.

Hagelgans, Nancy L. *et al*. *A Practical Guide to Cooperative Learning in Collegiate Mathematics*. MAA Notes Series, No. 37. Washington, DC: The Mathematical Association of America, 1995.

Harel, G. and E. Dubinsky. *The Concept of Function: Aspects of Epistemology and Pedagogy*, MAA Notes, No. 25. Washington, DC: The Mathematical Association of America, 1992.

Hendrix, Gertrude. Learning by Discovery, *The Mathematics Teacher*, 54 (May), 1961: 290–299.

Hertz-Lazarowitz, R. and N. Miller (editors). *Interaction in Cooperative Groups: The Theoretical Anatomy of Group Learning*. New York: Cambridge University Press, 1992.

Johnson, David and Roger Johnson. *Creative Conflict*. Edina, MN: Interaction Book Company, 1987.

Johnson, David and Roger Johnson. *Cooperation and Competition: Theory and Research.* Edina, MN: Interaction Book Company, 1989.

Johnson, David and Roger Johnson. *Leading the Cooperative School.* Edina, MN: Interaction Book Company, 1989.

Johnson, David, Roger Johnson and Karl Smith. *Active Learning: Cooperation in the College Classroom.* Edina, MN: Interaction Book Co, 1991.

Johnson, David W *et al.* Cooperative Learning: Increasing College Faculty Instructional Productivity. *ASHE-ERIC Higher Education Report*, No. 4. Washington, DC: The George Washington University School of Education and Human Development, 1991.

Jones, Phillip. Discovery Teaching: From Socrates to Modernity, *The Mathematics Teacher*, 63 (6), 1970: 501–508.

Kagan, Spencer. The Structural Approach to Cooperative Learning. *Educational Leadership*, 47 (4), 1989–90: 12–15.

Kagan, Spencer. *Cooperative Learning.* San Juan Capistrano, CA: Kagan Cooperative Learning Co., 1992.

Kagan, Spencer. *Cooperative Learning Resources for Teachers.* San Juan Capistrano, CA: Kagan Cooperative Learning Co., 1993.

Kaput, J. and E. Dubinsky. *Research Issues in Undergraduate Mathematics Learning*, MAA Notes, No. 33. Washington, DC: The Mathematical Association of America, 1994.

Kroll, Diana, Joanne Massingila, and Sue Mau. Grading Cooperative Problem Solving. *The Mathematics Teacher*, 85 (8), 1992.

Lyman, L. and H. Foyle. *Cooperative Grouping for Interactive Learning: Students, Teachers and Administrators.* Washington, DC: National Education Association, 1990.

Matthews, R., J. Cooper, N. Davidson, and P. Hawkes. Building Bridges Between Cooperative and Collaborative Learning, *Change: The Magazine of Higher Learning.* 27 (4), 1995: 34–40.

McKeen, R. and N. Davidson. An Alternative to Individual Instruction in Mathematics, *American Mathematical Monthly.* 82 (10), 1975: 1006–1009.

Michaelson Larry K. *Team Learning: A Comprehensive Approach for Harnessing the Power of Small Groups in Higher Education.* Vol. 11 in *To Improve the Academy*, 1992.

Millis, Barbara and Phil Cottell. *Cooperative Learning for Higher Education Faculty.* Phoenix, AZ: Oryx Press, 1998.

Moise, Edwin E. Five Views of the "New Math." Washington, DC: Council for Basic Education, Occasional papers, No. 8, 1965.

Myerscough, D. *et al.* Cryptography: Cracking Codes. *The Mathematics Teacher*, 743–750, 756–757.

National Council of Teachers of Mathematics. *Curriculum and Evaluation Standards for School Mathematics*, Reston, VA: 1989.

National Council of Teachers of Mathematics, *Principles and Standards for School Mathematics*, Reston, VA: 2000.

Newmann, F. and J. Thompson. *Effects of Cooperative Learning on Achievement in Secondary Schools: A Summary of Research.* Madison, WI: National Center on Effective Secondary Schools, 1987.

Parker, Ruth. *Mathematical Power: Lessons from a Classroom.* Portsmouth, NH: Heinemann, 1993.

Polya, George. *Mathematical Discovery*, Vols. 1 and 2. New York: Wiley, 1962, 1965.

Reid, J., P. Forrestal, and J. Cook. *Small Group Learning in the Classroom.* Chalkface Press; Portsmouth, NH: Heinemann, 1990.

Rossman, Alan J. and J. Barr von Oehsen. *Workshop Statistics: Discovery with Data and the Graphing Calculator.* New York: Springer, 1997.

Roy, P. *Cooperative Learning Groups: Students Learning Together.* Richfield, MN: Patricia Roy Company, 1990.

Schmuck, Richard and Patricia Schmuck. *Group Processes in the Classroom*, 7th ed. Madison, WI: Brown & Benchmark Publishers, 1997.

Bibliography

Schoenfeld, A. *Mathematical Problem Solving*. Orlando, FL: Academic Press, 1985.

Schoenfeld, Alan (editor). *Student Assessment in Calculus*. MAA Notes, No. 43. Washington, DC: The Mathematical Association of America, 1997.

Sharan, S. Cooperative Learning in Small Groups: Recent Methods and Effects on Achievement, Attitudes, and Ethnic Relations, *Review of Educational Research*, 50, 1980: 241–271.

Sharan, S. *Cooperative Learning: Theory and Research*. Westport, CT: Praeger Publishers, 1990.

Sharan, Shlomo (editor). *Handbook of Cooperative Learning Methods*. Westport, CT: Greenwood, 1993.

Sharan, S. and R. Hertz-Lazarowitz. *A Group Investigation Method of Cooperative Learning in the Classroom*. In *Cooperation in Education*, edited by S. Sharan, P. Hare, C. Webb, and R. Hertz-Lazarowitz, Provo, UT: Brigham Young University Press, 1980, pp. 14–46.

Sharan, S. and R. Hertz-Lazarowitz. Effects of an Instructional Change Program on Teachers' Behavior, Attitudes, and Perceptions, *Journal of Applied Behavioral Science* 18, 1982: 185–201.

Sharan, Yael and Shlomo Sharan. *Expanding Cooperative Learning Through Group Investigation*. New York: Teachers College Press, 1992.

Shulman, Lee and I. R. Keisler. *Learning by Discovery: A Critical Appraisal*, Rand McNally, 1966, 2nd ed. 1968.

Shulman, Lee. Psychological Controversies in the Teaching of Mathematics. In *Readings in Secondary School Mathematics*, edited by Douglas B. Aichele and Robert E. Reys. Boston, MA: Prindle, Weber, & Schmidt, 1971, 2nd ed. 1977.

Slavin, R. E. *Cooperative Learning*. New York: Longman, 1983.

Slavin, R. When Does Cooperative Learning Increase Student Achievement? *Psychological Bulletin*, 94, 1983: 429–445.

Slavin, R. Research on Cooperative Learning: Consensus and Controversy, *Educational Leadership*, 47, (4), 1989–90: 52–55.

Slavin, Robert. *Cooperative Learning: Theory, Research, and Practice*. Englewood Cliffs, NJ: Prentice Hall, 1990.

Slavin, Robert, *et al.* (editors). *Learning to Cooperate, Cooperating to Learn*. New York: Plenum Press, 1985.

Smith, Barbara L. and Jean MacGregor. What is Collaborative Learning? In *Collaborative Learning: A Sourcebook for Higher Education*, edited by A. Goodsell, M. Moher, and V. Tinte. University Park, PA: National Center on Postsecondary Teaching, Learning, and Assessment, 1992.

Solomon, R. D. and E. C. L. Solomon. *The Handbook for the Fourth R: Relationship Skills, Vol. 1, Relationship Skills*. Columbia, MD: National Institute for Relationship Training, 1987.

Solomon, R. D. and E. C. L. Solomon. *The Handbook for the Fourth R: Relationship Skills, Vol. 2, Relationship Skills for Group Discussion and Process*. Columbia, MD: National Institute for Relationship Training, 1987.

Solomon, R. D. and E. C. L. Solomon. *The Handbook for the Fourth R: Relationship Skills, Vol. 3, Relationship Activities for Cooperative and Collegial Learning*. Columbia, MD: National Institute for Relationship Training, 1993.

Springer, Leonard, Mary Elizabeth Stanne, and Samuel S. Donovan. Effects of Small-Group Learning on Undergraduates in Science, Mathematics, Engineering, and Technology: A Meta-Analysis. *Review of Educational Research*, 69 (1), 1999: 21–51.

Steffe, Leslie P. and Charles Smock. Model for Learning and Teaching Mathematics. In *Research on Mathematical Thinking of Young Children*, edited by L. P. Steffe. Reston, Va: National Council of Teachers of Mathematics, 1975.

Thompson, A. G., Teachers' Beliefs and Conceptions: A Synthesis of the Research, In *Handbook of Research on Mathematics Teaching and Learning*, edited by Douglas A. Grouws, New York: Macmillan, 1992.

Treisman, Uri. A Study of the Mathematical Performance of Black Students at the University of California, Berkeley. Thesis, University of California, Berkeley, 1985.

Tucker, Thomas W. (editor). *Priming the Calculus Pump: Innovations and Resources.* Prepared by the CUPM Subcommittee on Calculus Reform and the First Two Years. MAA Notes, No. 17. Washington, DC: The Mathematical Association of America, 1990.

University of Maryland Mathematics Project (UMMAP). *Unifying Concepts and Processes in Elementary Mathematics.* Boston: Allyn and Bacon, 1978.

Webb, Noreen. Task-Related Verbal Interaction and Mathematics Learning in Small Groups. *Journal for Research in Mathematics Education,* 22 (5), 1991: 366–389.

Weissglass, Julian. *Mathematics for Elementary Teaching: A Small-Group Approach for Teaching.* Dubuque, IA: Kendall-Hunt, 1990.

Weissglass, Julian. Small Group Learning. *The American Mathematical Monthly,* 100 (7), 1993: 662–668.

Weller, K. *et al.* An Examination of Student Performance Data in Recent APOS-Based Papers, in review.

II. Textbooks and Resource Materials for Cooperative Learning

Aliaga, Martha and Brenda Gunderson. *Interactive Statistics.* Upper Saddle River, NJ: Prentice Hall, 1999.

Barnes, Mary. *Investigating Change: An Introduction to Calculus for Australian Schools.* Carlton, South Victoria: Curriculum Corporation, Key Curriculum Press, Berkeley, CA: 1991.

Bassarear, Tom. *Mathematics for Elementary School Teachers.* Boston: Houghton Mifflin, 1997. (Accompanying *Explorations* volume has group activities.)

Baxter, Nancy, Ed Dubinsky, and G. Levin. *Learning Discrete Mathematics with ISETL.* New York: Springer-Verlag, 1989.

Becerra, Linda, Ongard Sirisaengtaksin, and Bill Waller. *College Algebra from a Unified Laboratory Perspective,* Detroit: Brooks/Cole, 1998.

Cannon, Lawrence O. and Joseph Elich, *Precalculus.* New York: Harper Collins College Publishers, 1994.

Carlson, Ronald and Mary Jean Winter. *Algebra Experiments II: Exploring Non-Linear Functions.* Menlo Park, CA: Addison-Wesley, 1993.

Chakerian, G. D., Dalvin D. Crabill, and Sherman K. Stein. *Geometry: A Guided Inquiry* . Pleasantville, NY: Sunburst, 1986.

Charles, Randall *et al. Problem-Solving Experiences in Algebra.* Menlo Park, CA: Addison-Wesley, 1991.

Charles, Randall *et al. Problem-Solving Experiences in Geometry* . Menlo Park, CA: Addison-Wesley, 1991.

Cohen, M. S., *et al.* (editors). *Student Research Projects in Calculus.* Washington, DC: The Mathematical Association of America, 1991.

Connected Curriculum Project, Duke University. *http://www.math.duke.edu/education/ccp/* 26 August 1999.

Dancis, Jerome. Linear Algebra. University of Maryland, Mathematics Department, College Park, MD, 40742.

Davidson, Neil and Frances Gulick. *Abstract Algebra: An Active Learning Approach,* Boston: Houghton Mifflin, 1976.

Davidson, Neil, and Frances Gulick. Instructor's Manual for Abstract Algebra: An Active Learning Approach, Houghton Miflin Company, Boston, 1976.

DeMarois, Phil, Mercedes McGowen, and Darlene Whitkanack. *Applying Algebraic Thinking to Data: Concepts and Processes for the Intermediate Algebra Student.* New York: Harper Collins, 1996.

Dubinsky, Ed and Uri Leron. *Learning Abstract Algebra with ISETL.* New York: Springer-Verlag, 1994.

Dubinsky, Ed, Keith E. Schwingendorf, and David M. Mathews. *Calculus, Concepts,*

Bibliography

and Computers, 2nd ed. New York: McGraw-Hill, 1995.

Edwards, C. Henry and David E. Penney. *Calculus with Analytic Geometry*, 5th ed. Upper Saddle River, NJ: Prentice Hall, 1998.

Fendel, Dan, Diane Resek, Lynne Alper, and Sherry Fraser. *Interactive Mathematics Program* (*IMP*). Berkeley, CA: Key Curriculum Press, 1996.

Fenton, William E. and Ed Dubinsky. *Introduction to Discrete Mathematics with ISETL*. New York: Springer-Verlag, 1996.

Fraga, R. (editor). *Calculus Problems for a New Century*. MAA Notes, No. 28. Washington, DC: The Mathematical Association of America, 1993.

Gallian, Joseph A. *Contemporary Abstract Algebra*, 4th ed. Boston: Houghton Mifflin, 1998.

Halpin, Pat. *A Laboratory Approach to Introductory Calculus*. New York: McGraw Hill, 1994.

Hastings, Nancy Baxter. *Workshop Calculus*. New York: Springer, 1997.

Hastings, Nancy Baxter and Barbara E. Reynolds. *Workshop Calculus with Graphing Calculators*. New York: Springer, 1999.

Herr, Ted and Ken Johnson. *Problem Solving Strategies: Crossing The River With Dogs*. Berkeley, CA: Key Curriculum Press, 1994.

Hirsch, Christian *et al*. *Contemporary Mathematics in Context: A Unified Approach* (*Core-Plus Mathematics Project*). Chicago, IL: Janson, 1997.

Holder, Leonard Irvin, James DeFranza, and Jay M. Passachoff. *Calculus*. Pacific Grove, CA: Brooks/Cole, 1994.

Jackson, M. B. and J. R. Ramsey (editors). *Problems for Student Investigations*. MAA Notes, Vol.30. Washington, DC: The Mathematical Association of America, 1993.

Jacobs, Harold R. *Mathematics: A Human Endeavor*, 3rd edition. New York: Freeman, 1994.

Johnson, Jerry and Benny Evans. *Discovering Calculus with Derive*, 2nd ed. New York: Wiley, 1995.

Lay, David C. *Linear Algebra and Its Applications*, 2nd ed. Menlo Park, CA: Addison-Wesley, 2000.

Martin-Gay, K. Elayn. *Intermediate Algebra*. Upper Saddle River, NJ: Prentice Hall, 1999.

Martin-Gay, K. Elayn. *Introductory Algebra*. Upper Saddle River, NJ: Prentice Hall, 1999.

Mathews, D. *Precalculus Investigations using Derive*. New York: Harper Collins, 1994.

Mathews, David M. and Keith E. Schwingendorf. *Precalculus Investigations using MapleV*. New York: Harper Collins, 1994.

Meyer, Carol and Tom Sallee. *Make It Simpler. A Practical Guide to Problem Solving in Mathematics*. Menlo Park, CA: Addison-Wesley, 1983.

Miles, Thomas J. and Douglas W. Nance. *Mathematics: One of the Liberal Arts*. Pacific Grove, CA: Brooks/Cole, 1997.

Moran, Judy Flagg, Marsha Davis, and Mary Murphy. *Precalculus: Concepts in Context*. Pacific Grove, CA: Brooks/Cole, 1996.

Murdock, Jerald, Ellen Kamischke, and Eric Kamischke. *Algebra Through Data Exploration: A Graphing Calculator Approach*. Berkeley, CA: Key Curriculum Press, 1996.

Posamentier, Alfred S. and Gordon Sheridan. *Math Motivators: Investigations in Geometry*. Menlo Park, CA: Addison-Wesley, 1982.

Reynolds, Barbara E. *et al*. *Precalculus, Concepts and Computers*. New York: McGraw Hill, 1996.

Rossman, Alan J. *Workshop Statistics: Discovery with Data*. New York: Springer, 1996.

Rossman, Alan J. and Beth Chance. *Workshop Statistics: Discovery with Data and Minitab*. New York: Springer, 1998.

Rossman, Alan J. and J. Barr von Oehsen. *Workshop Statistics: Discovery with Data and the Graphing Calculator*. New York: Springer, 1997.

Schaufele, Christopher and Nancy Zumoff. *Earth Algebra: College Algebra with Applications to Environmental Issues*, 2nd ed. Menlo Park, CA: Addison-Wesley, 1999.

Schwartz, Diane Driscoll. *Conjecture and Proof: An Introduction to Mathematical Thinking*. Fort Worth, TX: Saunders, 1997.

Serra, Michael. *Discovery Geometry: An Inductive Approach*, 2nd ed. Berkeley, CA: Key Curriculum Press, 1996.

Smith, D. A. and L. C. Moore. *Calculus: Modeling and Application* (with supplements). Heath, 1996.

Solow, Anita E. (editor). *Learning by Discovery: A Lab Manual for Calculus*. MAA Notes, No. 27. Washington, DC: The Mathematical Association of America, 1993.

Starfield, Anthony M., Karl Smith, and Andrew Bleloch. *How to Model It: Problem Solving for the Computer Age*. Edina, MN: Burgess International Group, 1994.

Stein, Sherman and Calvin Crabill. *Elementary Algebra: A Guided Inquiry*. Pleasantville, NY: Sunburst, 1986.

Stein, S. K., C. D. Crabill, and G. D. Chakerian. *Algebra II Trigonometry: A Guided Inquiry*. Pleasantville, NY: Sunburst, 1986.

Stewart, James. *Calculus*, 4th ed. Pacific Grove, CA: Brooks/Cole, 1999.

Straffin, P. (editor). *Applications of Calculus*. MAA Notes, No. 29. Washington, DC: The Mathematical Association of America, 1993.

University of Maryland Mathematics Project (UMMAP). *Unifying Concepts and Processes in Elementary Mathematics*. Boston: Allyn and Bacon, 1978.

Wiebe, Arthur *et al*. *Project AIMS*. Fresno, CA: AIMS Education Foundation, 1982-1988.

Winter, Mary and Ronald Carlson. *Algebra Experiments I: Exploring Linear Functions*. Menlo Park, CA: Addison-Wesley, 1993.